# ESCAPE FROM
# MANAGEMENT
# HELL

# ESCAPE FROM
# MANAGEMENT
# HELL

## 12 Tales of Horror, Humor, and Heroism

## ROBERT D. GILBREATH

Berrett-Koehler Publishers
San Francisco

Berrett-Koehler Publishers, Inc.
155 Montgomery St.
San Francisco, CA 94104-4109

**Ordering Information**

*Orders by individuals and organizations.* Berrett-Koehler publications are available through bookstores or can be ordered direct from the publisher at the Berrett-Koehler address above or by calling (800) 929-2929.

*Quantity sales.* Berrett-Koehler publications are available at special quantity discounts when purchased in bulk by corporations, associations, and others. For details, write to the "Special Sales Department" at the Berrett-Koehler address above or call (415) 288-0260.

*Orders by U.S. trade bookstores and wholesalers.* Please contact Publishers Group West, 4065 Hollis Street, Box 8843, Emeryville, CA 94608; tel. (800) 788-3123; fax (510) 658-1834.

*Orders for college textbook/course adoption use.* Please contact Berrett-Koehler Publishers. 155 Montgomery St., San Francisco, CA 94104-4109; tel. (415) 288-0260; fax (415) 362-2512.

**Printed in the United States of America**

Printed on acid-free and recycled paper that meets the strictest state and U. S. guidelines for recycled paper (50 percent recycled waste, including 10 percent postconsumer waste).

**Library of Congress Cataloging-in-Publication Data**

Gilbreath, Robert D. (Robert Dean), 1949-
      Escape from management hell : twelve tales of horror, humor and heroism /
Robert D. Gilbreath, — 1st ed.
        p.    cm.
     ISBN 1-881052-26-5 (alk. paper) : $19.95
     1. Management. I. Title.
HD31.G4953   1993
658—dc20                        93-6596
                                               CIP

First Edition
    *First Printing 1993*

Cover and chapter illustrations: Dilleen Marsh
Book design and production: Clear Communication/The Graphic Solution

Every successful escapist
requires an accomplice.
Thank-you, Linda.

# CONTENTS

# PREFACE

The best way to detect a pattern is to step away from the isolated points of experience and view them from a distance. Then, the individual dots start to connect, to form a picture. For many of us, this happens when a sudden, unexpected event takes us away from the pressures and pace of work.

It might be an accident or illness, a vacation, or something as simple as missing a plane and having to wait, and to think. That's the key—to think. Or, more precisely, to ponder. So much of what we do in business that passes for thinking is really information processing, reacting, acting out roles by reflex or through habit. When chance or change forces us to step back and ponder, the implications of what we're doing often stand out in sharp relief. The dots connect themselves. The picture becomes manifest.

Today, chance and change are forcing millions of us to reconsider what management is. The dots in the picture include working with fewer people and with greater demands. Watching friends and colleagues depart under abrupt and sometimes arbitrary circumstances. Asking disloyal subordinates to believe in your goals, while at the same time having your superiors try to change or circumvent them. Being told to serve the customer and worship quality, and yet squeeze as much profit out of the market as you can get—and fast. Is the picture starting to come into focus?

It is a picture of Hell—Management Hell. A place where the rules are changing so fast that what was once a career climb is now a free fall. What was challenging is now chaotic. What was trying is now tortuous. What made sense is now bizarre. What was unthink-able is now the norm—if "norm" has any meaning at all anymore. Management Hell.

With this book I hope to pull you out of your Management Hell, away from the daily inconsistencies and turmoil long enough for that clear picture to emerge—for the implications to take shape, and, hopefully, for you to see your way out. *Escape from Management Hell* is more than a book title. It should be your personal and profes-sional goal.

Tom Brokaw, anchor for the NBC Nightly News, once remarked that no matter what the news of the day, no matter how appalling or trivial, the first thing the audience will notice is your tie.

I've seen the same phenomenon firsthand. No matter how many seminars I conduct, and I've done more than two hundred in over twenty-five countries, the first and last thing the audience will remember are the stories. It doesn't matter how significant or minor the lessons, how detailed or inflammatory the discussions that fol-low. They'll remember the stories years after the points I've strug-gled to make are forgotten.

So scan through the contents of this book, and you'll see this point hasn't been lost on me. You won't find laundry lists of key facts, bullet slides, or flowcharts. Though this is a book for business managers, you won't find case studies of excellent corporations, either. I know these are as impermanent as dust in the wind.

Stories last. Especially if they involve people in predicaments that reflect yours. People struggling with dramatically new and chal-lenging issues. People caught in ethical dilemmas and grappling with the irrepressible phenomenon of our time: change. People you'll recognize immediately, because you've dealt with them before.

In this book, they'll be dressed in exotic clothes, they'll be situated in strange surroundings. This may seem, at first, to place them at a distance, perhaps risking irrelevancy. But it may bring objectivity, new perspectives that yield startling insights. When we're too close to the everyday, we often lose this vantage—we need to escape our own management hells to see just how magnificent and maddening they truly are.

Among the scoundrels and the saints, you'll spot the boss that almost ruined your career, or helped make it. You'll see the customer you lost, the competitor you fought. The wise men or women who set you on the right track. The rivals who tried to push you from it.

Along the way you might encounter someone else. Someone who realizes that work is full of triumphs and tragedies and has shared both. Someone who still struggles, day-by-day, to make sense out of this brutal, sometimes boring, yet often surprisingly satisfying world of business. Maybe you'll recognize a mentor, maybe a colleague; but, more likely, that someone will be you.

Duluth, Georgia                                    Robert D. Gilbreath
January 1993

# THE AUTHOR

Robert Gilbreath is president of Change Management for Philip Crosby Associates, Inc., in Atlanta, Georgia. He leads its worldwide practice and is responsible for change training, planning, and implementation services for clients in thirty-five countries.

He is the author of four previous books, including *Save Yourself!* and *Forward Thinking* (McGraw-Hill). His *Winning Through Change* videos, produced by the American Management Association, are used by over five hundred major corporations, governments and institutions. He has presented more than two hundred seminars to business executives dealing with strategic and operational transformations taking place in today's global market.

Gilbreath founded the Organization Change practice of Andersen Consulting, has been a columnist for *New Management*, and has written for *The Journal of Business Strategy, The Atlanta Journal Constitution, The Los Angeles Business Journal* and *The International Finance* and *Law Review*. He has been featured in *U.S. News and World Report*, the *Washington Post*, and interviewed on the CNN, ABC, and NBC networks, as well as the CBS Evening News with Dan Rather.

For more than twenty years, Gilbreath has helped clients meet the challenges of structural and organizational change in Japan, Spain, England, Switzerland, Argentina, Brazil, Italy, Finland, Singapore, Norway, Canada, Mexico, Australia, South Africa, and many other countries. His clients have included IBM, the U.S. Postal Service, Phillips Petroleum, Johnson & Johnson, Carnation,

Firestone, General Motors, the government of Great Britain, and the Engineering Advancement Association of Japan. He has lectured at Harvard University Graduate School of business, Massachusetts Institute of Technology (Sloan School of Management), Pennsylvania State University, and the University of Mexico.

Educated at the U.S. Military Academy at West Point, the University of Kentucky, and the University of Tennessee, Robert and his wife, Linda, live outside Atlanta. Their son, Bob, studies economics at Duke University and their daughter, Alice, is a biomedical engineering student at Vanderbilt University.

# PROLOGUE

*On the afternoon of Monday, the 17th, amid a gathering snowstorm, a twin engine commuter jet ascended from a mountain strip and climbed into the skies over the Rockies. Aboard were twelve passengers, all executives of major corporations, all having recently completed a leadership conference held in an exclusive ski resort.*

*They had convened the previous Friday, carrying skis and boots and expensive snow fashions, flown in on the four winds at company expense. After a two-hour cocktail reception, an obscure professor stood at a lectern and began to describe management principles. His silver-haired assistant, shoulders hunched by years of pain, manned the slide projector from the rear of the room. Leadership principles shot through the lens of the machine and illuminated a makeshift screen.*

*Ten minutes into this lecture, the executives grew noticeably restless and disinterested. The professor raised his voice mildly, attempting to continue with his key points. Their attention and respect fell proportionately.*

*At the rear of the room one openly perused the stock quotations of* The Wall Street Journal. *Another unsnapped his briefcase on the table before him and began whispering into a micro-recorder—dictating a memo he'd put off days ago.*

*As the speaker turned his back to the group to address a chart on the screen, a front-row manager spun around to those behind him and mimed a suppressed yawn. Chuckles rippled among those who noticed. Another whispered to his neighbor, saying, "Fairy Tales!*

*Nothing but stories for children!"*

*The professor continued, absorbed in his presentation. But when he turned from the screen, he couldn't help notice three empty seats near the rear exit. They were leaving now, one by one, every time his back was turned. Snow was beginning to fall outside the window. Soon the slopes would be perfect. Those still seated looked longingly out the windows, and began squirming and taking exaggerated glances at their wristwatches.*

*Defeated, the professor asked his silver-haired assistant to extinguish the projector's lamp. In the ensuing darkness, nothing but screeching table legs and shuffling feet could be heard. The exit door swung open and the stragglers departed, scurrying off to their private pleasures.*

*The forgotten professor slunk among the shadows, felt his way behind the screen, and disappeared, leaving his assistant with the chore of apologizing to a final executive and escorting her to the door.*

*Perhaps this last holdout left thinking the speaker was sulking in shame, hiding behind the curtain—a failure, totally out of touch, totally irrelevant.*

*But he was none of these. Nor was he sulking or shameful. He was thinking, fuming, steaming, planning, and plotting. When he heard the door close and his assistant approach the curtain, he called out in a surprisingly confident voice.*

*"Have they all left?" he asked.*

*"Yes sir, all twelve. And sir . . . ?"*

*"What is it?"*

*"If it's any consolation, I'm sorry. This was my idea, after all."*

*"Don't reflect on it for a single moment," came the startlingly altered voice from behind the screen. "I have other ways of teaching, more effective ways. Venues that are less comforting, and confrontations unavoidable. Don't worry about the audience," he*

*scoffed. "To hell with them, anyway!"*

*By that time, the executives had already rushed to their suites, doffed their travel clothes, and donned down and lycra. Some hit the slopes with the ferocity of shore-starved sailors seeking a portside tavern. Others organized high-stakes poker games. Some dashed to their rooms and embraced their telephones, contacting their voice mail systems with the ardor of reunited lovers. And still others plunged into a swirling whirlpool, their bodies and thoughts disappearing in steam and surrender. All forgot the professor, and his assistant, and whatever it was he was trying to teach them.*

*Thus the long weekend was spent by some of the world's most powerful. At its conclusion, some were tanned from the sharp sunlight of the crystal and sugar slopes. Some were richer, some poorer. Some were rubbing knees begging for just one more hour in the whirlpool. Others jittered in their expensive business suits—visibly anxious to get back to the heat and excitement of the corporate chase.*

*They met at the small general aviation hanger, boarded a commuter jet, reclined in their seats, and settled down for the short flight to Denver.*

*In the air traffic control tower at Stapleton, the small craft first appeared as a swift-moving, steady blip. A young controller monitored the screen with one eye and watched the growing size and frequency of snowflakes out a smeared plate glass window with the other. Snowbirds going home, he whispered to himself, then crushed a paper coffee cup and hurled it across the small deck toward an overflowing basket. The wad of wet pulp careened off a gray metal desk adjacent to the can, bounced against a cream colored cinder block wall, and plopped into the cylinder. Satisfied, the controller returned his attention to the screen, the snowbirds, the approaching radar blip. It had disappeared.*

3

*He punched resolution adjusters, jolted into an adrenaline rush, rubbed his eyes, and pulled his metal chair closer to the screen. AspenAir 409 had vanished.*

*Distracting new blips emerged from the screen's borders and into view, more planes homing in on Denver like moths drawn to a flame. More trajectories to control, more people to safeguard. But where was AspenAir 409?*

*Panic is contagious. In a few seconds two supervisors huddled over the controller's shoulder, simultaneously chiding and helping. As if someone had elevated the temperature one hundred degrees all at once, the three men desperately began to shout and sweat. One of them snatched the microphone and radioed a frantic message into the chilly, whitening atmosphere. "AspenAir 409, this is Stapleton, over? AspenAir 409, this is Stapleton. We have lost contact, over."*

*Cackling static poured through the speaker and frosted their hearts. Silence heavy as lead. More buttons were punched, heads scratched, recriminations launched.*

*"Twelve VIPs were on that flight," muttered the controller. He fought back the gallows humor. He fought back the urge to ask his supervisor if they would be saved by their golden parachutes. He resisted the impulse to ask his colleagues if the impending crash would force their respective stocks to plunge or climb. He simply sat there, his supervisor's nervous breath warming the back of his neck, and wondered, "Where in hell are they?"*

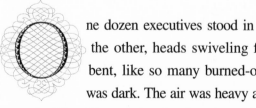ne dozen executives stood in a loose line, one behind the other, heads swiveling from side to side, backs bent, like so many burned-out business travelers. It was dark. The air was heavy and foul, reeking with the stench of fear. They squinted and squirmed in unaccustomed anguish.

An iron chain ran through all twelve, linking the manacles on their right hands. When one would shift, raise a hand to wipe a sweating brow or loosen a tie, the rest would jerk in reflex, and groan at the offender.

Some were midwestern industrialists. You could tell this by their football shoulders and their thick-soled, sensible brougham wing tips. By their beer guts and no nonsense suits. Steel men, autos, rubber, pork belly futures.

The ones shifting their weight from side to side, uttering little oooh's and ahhh's as they did were undoubtedly New York or London financiers—their thin Swiss Bally pumps transmitting the floor's heat with all the efficiency of aluminum. Raiders, greenmailers, arbitragers, margin hunters. Their pocket scarves, glossy silk and cheerful, slid across their faces in a vain attempt to stanch the perspiration. Fashionable, to be sure, but not practical—not here.

Scattered among them was the occasional California real estate speculator, airline tycoon, chief financial officer, board chairman. And, of course, backstabbers, frauds, cheats, yes men, schmoozers, name-droppers, influence peddlers, liars, and double-crossers, too. That these don't add up to twelve is no surprise. Most qualified in more than one category.

Orange and red lights jumped and flashed at their sides, animating the cavern walls, giving shape and motion to the shadows that danced there. The group shifted and the chain clanked. Muttered curses dispersed among them.

Hissing sounds like ventilated steam sighed from the cavernous roof. The labored, marching strokes of a wheezing bellows could be heard from somewhere off in the darkness. The vibrating rock floor grew hotter and began to glow.

Cashmere scarves, calfskin gloves, silk neckwear—the accouterments of success——flew from the line as fast as the executives could wrestle them off. They vainly fought off overcoats and Italian suit jackets. Once folded cautiously by flight attendants and hung in first-class exclusivity, these now hung from their chained arms, twisted, inside out, the dross of past excess.

They kept their shoes. The floor was cracking, and little plumes of pressurized vapor sputtered through the fissures. Snapping blue arcs of electricity twitched around and about, tracing mocking veins of power and light.

Condensed steam rolled down the sweating walls and sizzled off the floor. Clouds of stench attacked them. Decay was in the air. And death. And doom. Despair would come later, once they realized where they were. And why. And what it would take to escape.

A tiny plaque bolted to the flickering stone wall told them they were on level twelve, sub-basement. Jostling about and looking over their shoulders, they began to converse.

"Level twelve? Hey, this must be the parking garage! Anybody seen a black Mercedes? Connecticut plates?"

"Quit yanking the chain, will ya? I got a tennis elbow's killing me already."

"Remind me never to fly commercial again!"

"Where the hell's the phones around here? I gotta check my messages."

"What do you have to do to get a drink in this place, anyway? Beg?"

Suddenly a booming voice howled from the darkness: "No need to beg!" The response was so unexpected and the voice so hideous that they each yanked the chain and pressed their hands over their ears in pain and fright. Searing flames leaped to their front, while superheated steam billowed from a gaping wound in the rock's face. A huge figure stepped out, silhouetted by the incandescent backlight of a roaring furnace. A corona of charcoal-winged creatures erupted from his head and exploded into the darkness, flapping away like a death rattle.

He seemed a man, old and hunched at the shoulders. But it was difficult to tell for certain, for he was wearing a silver suit. Flares and flickers reflected off the shiny material, much like the flame-proof uniform of a steelworker or the protective suit of a firefighter. A heavy metal dome, a welder's mask, protected the head, and from behind a narrow rectangle of thick smoked glass two ruby points of light stabbed outwards at them. When he turned to scan the captives, the smoke glass cleared and they could see flowing silver hair within. Then came the voice, the Darth Vader tonal moan, half breathing, half disgust.

"Begging is commonplace here," he began. "It will get you nowhere."

All eyes fixed on the speaker as all hearts stopped, waiting. No one dared move or speak. He stepped closer. "Please allow me to introduce myself. I am Reflecto!" he announced proudly, "Satan's chief operating officer. And as I've said, begging will get you nowhere.

"You are in Hell, fools! You are expected to beg! Kings and princes, artists, Hollywood superstars, real estate magnates, sports legends—they all beg down here. Hell has a way of doing that, of bringing out a surfeit of humility.

"But this is not your regular, first-class hell, my friends," he continued. "Look around. You'll find no princes or paupers here, no stars, no heroes, no legends of sport. They have their own places. This, my friends, is solely for your souls." Then he sneered audibly and raised his arms, spreading his hands expansively about. "Welcome to Management Hell!"

Just then an impetuous prisoner shouted loudly from somewhere in the center of the linked sufferers. "Money, then! If begging won't get me out, I'll pay!" And he reached into his hip pocket and withdrew his billfold, hoping to flash a little American Express gold—perhaps wishing to upgrade, even if it was just to Purgatory. But the eel skin cover was smoking, and rivulets of melting plastic scalded his fingers. He flung the wallet away and screamed in pain.

"No!" roared the figure in the silver suit, "Money is worthless to me. It burns a hole in my pocket!" He cackled at his own joke, snickered, and tapped his heavy shining boot on the brimstone. The linked executives trembled and glanced nervously at each other. Never had they confronted such a response. Money is worthless? They were dumfounded, helpless. A mild man, perhaps once an accountant, peered up from them and put forth a modest request.

"What then," he inquired, "would you have us do?"

"It is not money," the shining suit replied, his voice lowered, his words deliberate as they resonated from behind the welder's mask like they were coming from the end of a thousand-mile-long corridor. "Nor is it sex or power or fame or security, or even a corner office. Neither do I require titles or limousines. I have no need for bonuses or stock options, nor do I value golden parachutes or handshakes of any kind."

They cowered and listened in amazement. This was, indeed, a novel and bewildering experience. This was, in fact, a thing for which they were totally unprepared. The speaker paused, then stamped a heavy boot and shook a shimmering gloved finger above his hooded head. "Wisdom!" he bellowed. "I must have wisdom!"

They cringed in unison and clumped together in terror at his pronouncement, for the word meant nothing to them. Wisdom? What is this, wisdom? No one spoke, for they were certain Satan's henchman would soon tell them.

"You know budgets and prices and costs," he lectured them. "You know chains of command and spans of control and sales and marketing, and you know how to interface and liaise and touch base and do lunch! You know how to put a positive spin on a disastrous project, how to doll up an annual report to make a stupid investment seem brilliant!" His voice was rising now, his temper elevating. "But!" he shouted, "you are here because you lack management wisdom! Your shortsightedness, your greed, your well-intentioned management styles, and your tried and true techniques just don't cut it anymore!" He waited for a response that never came.

"You just don't get it, do you?"

No one answered. They knew the monstrous thing wasn't expecting an answer. He was winding up now, and they were anxious to learn what this wisdom was, how to get it, and, most important, how to use it to get the hell out of there.

"There are twelve of you," the demon told them, "and there are twelve steps that take you to freedom. Each of you must earn your own way out of hell. Each of you must take one step. If all rise, all will escape. If one, if so much as one of you falters, you will all perish. Your fate is linked by wisdom, as firmly as iron now links your bodies."

"Why's that?" asked a prisoner. "Why can't we each make it on our own?"

"Damn you, because I said so!" bellowed Reflecto. "This isn't a resort, slime! You are not guests here, you are inmates. You can't check out whenever you like, do whatever you want, and offend whomever you please! This is Hell, idiot, not a hotel!"

Then the questioner replied, "Considering some of the places I've stayed, it's hard to tell one from the other."

Everyone winced at this brashness, expecting Reflecto's wrath to be swift and sure. But, amazingly, he laughed.

"You have a sense of humor," he said to the man. "That's good. That's very good. You see, to escape, to leave this inferno, you must amuse me and my boss. Each in a different way. You must teach us of your errors and triumphs, enlighten our feeble devil minds, if you will. You must impart management wisdom to us. And not drivel, not some 'how to swim with the sharks' bullshit! I have seen sharks beg, too!

"The evil one wants enduring, effective wisdom. He demands to know how to cope in today's world up there, under today's competitive conditions. For, as you can imagine, there is no one more competitive than my boss.

"And do not expect him to be the simple devil of your childhood nightmares, either. He is not a caricature, nor a cartoon. He is much more complex, his motives much deeper. My master is evil, yes, but he is also brilliant. In that regard, vermin, he is not unlike any of you. And, as you will soon learn, to see into hell you must see into yourselves.

"Teach the rancid rogue of quality, and change, and cost control. He lusts for the rules of innovation. You shall tell him of competitive advantage, management by participation, decentralization, empowerment, all that stuff!"

"Okay, Okay, we get it already," yelled an anxious prisoner, "just tell us how you want it, and we'll give it to you. Hey, we're easy. We'll buy it, we'll kidnap some professor and ship him to you Federal Express. We'll fax you a purchase order, whaddever he wants."

"He wants stories."

"Stories?" asked the distraught prisoner. "Stories?"

"Damn right!" shot the devil's assistant. "And not just any stories. Particular stories. Stories that demonstrate the folly and futility of your individual sins. Stories that repudiate your errors. That reflect deep remorse."

A distressed executive strained to move closer and spoke loudly:

"Have you heard the one about the three guys who walk into a bar and . . . "

"Shut up, fool! You haven't been listening! You are not in Aspen anymore, insects. You cannot laugh at wisdom here. You must feel it deeply, and share its intensity with me."

The group silenced, and Satan's assistant proceeded to describe the exercise.

"Each of you will be given a theme, a legal pad of paper, and a pencil. Each of you will be granted two weeks to compose a meaningful, entertaining, perhaps even amusing tale. Each of you must read the tale before my master, the devil himself. If every story pleases him, if he learns enduring lessons from each, you shall all be allowed to leave. That, worms, is how you escape from Management Hell!"

"Please!" shrieked an overwrought executive at the end of the line. "Please! Put me on the rack! Boil me in oil, toss me into a pit of wolves! Anything, I'll take any punishment you have! Just don't make me pick up a pencil and write something original! God, man, have you no pity?"

"Pity?" inquired the devil's assistant. "Pity? Not hardly, especially not for vermin like yourself. Patience—now that's what we have here. Plenty of patience. And you, captains of industry, financial wizards, empire builders, corporate chieftains?" He paused; they trembled. "You have two weeks."

With that a phalanx of silver-suited guards emerged from the shadows and hustled the chain of perspiring, shocked execs through a heavy steel door studded with glowing bolts and locks. This was the writing room: twelve tiny cubicles, each holding one battered battleship gray steel desk and a molded orange plastic waiting room chair. There are no perks in Management Hell.

Each prisoner was ushered to a cubicle and shoved down into a seat. The chain between them was cut. Ankle irons were then shackled to the desk legs.

Each stared glumly at a metal desktop. There, as promised, were the two tools of torture: pencil and paper. Across the top sheet of the pad each read a special assignment, a unique theme. Groans of recognition and despair rippled over the tops of the cubicles.

Then a sharp crack was heard, as an asbestos bullwhip snaked out from nowhere and popped over their heads. "Silence!" Reflecto wailed. "Nothing shall be heard but the sound of pencils scratching out your feeble notions!"

Twelve humbled executives thereupon faced the ultimate horror: a blank sheet of paper. The bullwhip cracked again, snapping in the spaces between their fevered minds. Twelve points of graphite bolted to life and raced across fields of canary yellow, dragging wisdom in their wake. The escape from Management Hell began.

# THE BONES OF HAMMURABI
## (MEET THE ORIGINAL CONTROL FREAK)

"In place of the rigid, ancient law, man must hereafter with free heart decide for himself what is good and what is evil."

—**Fyodor Dostoevski**, *The Grand Inquisitor*

*Prisoner number one was taken down a narrow corridor leading to a massive, ornate gateway. Rusted iron creaked when the guard moved a brass lever, and the gate swung open. Prisoner number one was kicked inside.*

*He sprawled on the sizzling stones and picked himself up, standing unsteadily, his hand clutching a sheaf of ratted yellow pages in a death grip. The devil was on a raised platform, behind a heavy curtain; but as prisoner number one looked up through the smoke and sulfurous vapors, he saw nothing. Then the devil spoke from on high.*

*"How does it feel to be an employee?" he asked, his voice surprisingly soft and calm.*

*"Employee?" the prisoner asked. "What do you mean?"*

*"You're in the dark, frightened. You are listening to orders from someone you don't know. You're down there, and I'm up here—hidden. Seem familiar?"*

*"You mean, does it have anything to do with how I conducted my business?" the terrified executive offered.*

*"Were you born stupid," the devil snorted, "or did you develop that deficiency in an MBA program? Of course that's what I mean!*

*You ran your company with an iron fist, didn't you? You issued orders and enforced control from the top of a pyramid of power. You isolated yourself. You ruled by edict. You were the classic top-down manager."*

"No company can run without a certain degree of control," suggested the chastened prisoner. Then he added this: "That was my job. I made the rules, and I enforced them."

"See where it got you?" asked the devil.

"Yes," mumbled the prisoner, looking down at his smoking shoes.

"Have you got a story for me, then? A story about control, power, law? A story that will undo the mistakes of a power freak in Hell?"

The prisoner held up the sheaf of papers and answered, "It is a story about bones, sir."

"Ooohhh!" came the response from behind the curtain. "I love it already! I hope it deals with death and destruction and cruelty and all that good stuff," squealed Satan.

"That it does," whispered the cowering executive.

"Then tell it, man!" shrieked the devil. "And," he lowered his voice and paused . . . "it better be good!"

Prisoner number one held the pad close to his face, for he was extremely nearsighted. The papers shook, and with a trembling voice he began.

his is a story about bones, and of similarity and difference. For management is a constant battle between the desire for each: consistency in approach across operations, versus flexibility and local adaptation. Great corporations have fought these civil wars—centralization vs. decentralization, uniformity vs. autonomy. And great leaders have had to determine, daily, when too much of either is fatal.

Hammurabi is known to history as the law-giver, the first

monarch to codify rules of behavior, and as such he is revered by many. This king of Babylon lived from 1792-50 B.C., and archaeologists have found his code. It is amazing in detail and specificity. It covers all conduct imaginable, from the price of chicken wings to the punishment for wearing a robe in a licentious manner.

Hammurabi was a control freak.

But in his day—and in his eyes—he was known as a great strategist, a man of principle, and unswerving in his dedication. This, we've been told, is the profile of a leader. This, we know, can be a formula for disaster.

"Tell the damned story!" screamed the devil. "Get to the death and destruction!"

Prisoner number one nervously cleared his throat, flipped over two pages, found a new starting place, and continued to read.

In Central Africa, far from each coast and hidden among the rain forest, lies a natural wonder, the origins of which are speculative. For it is a huge crater in the earth, filled with water, and fathoms deep. Some suggest a meteor collided with the earth eons ago. Some say it was the work of a fanatical race of devil worshipers, digging to find union with their anti-god. How it was created is still in question, but what it contains, down in the depths of its murky liquid, is now quite evident. It is filled with bones. The dark waters are sated with skeletons.

Thousand and thousands of them, of all ages, sexes, and occupations were discovered there by our aquatic archaeologists. They are not bound as in sacrifice or punishment, and they are not buried with ritual or surrounded by amulets or tokens for a journey to a new world. They lie at random, in great jumbled piles, as if they leapt like lemmings to the sea, into the silent pit in that jungle, at once. Why?

The secret must reside with the only written record among the mountains of underwater calcium, a fragment of stone among the bone. Water has washed away the inscription it once contained, but a corner is chiseled in a faraway script. That corner contains one word: *Hammurabi*. And that word leads us now to a land hundreds of miles to the northeast. Across Egypt, through the Levant, and on to the valley of the Tigris and the Euphrates. There we will find the cradle of civilization: Babylon. Perchance the answer lies there.

On the throne of Babylon sat Hammurabi, the master of Mesopotamia, the mouthpiece of Marduk, god of the world. And Hammurabi grew distressed that certain far-flung tribes in his domain did not send conscripts for the wars of domination; indeed, they fled his recruiters. So Hammurabi sent out the word. All peoples of all lands would dispatch their governors or representatives to Babylon. "We will have a meeting," he proclaimed.

So fearing the despot's terror, they came. They came from the Sudan and Egypt and Ethiopia. From Arabia, Persia, and along the shores of the gulf. And from the islands, too. A varietal assemblage of ambassadors, underlings, and territorial overlords, all serving Hammurabi and at the mercy of his armies. And once assembled in the great Hall of Commands, Hammurabi appeared, accompanied by his retinue of eunuchs.

The tyrant looked out and was aghast at the sight. There stood bronzed men, elegant in linen robes shot through with silver. And men in wild boar skins, bedecked with animal teeth and smeared with red ocher. Still others, from other lands, in tanned leather with closely barbered locks.

There were half-naked ones in attendance, attired only in loin cloths, with their long tresses tied in colorful ribbons. Others sported feathers, some had beards, and some were shaven. Some oiled, some powdered, some wrapped in fur, or swathed in silks. Each of the hundred varied in fashion and appearance according to local customs and climate. This upset Hammurabi. This is no empire, he thought, this is a motley crew.

So instead of haranguing them on the principles of conscription and demanding more men and horses to pursue his campaigns, Hammurabi expanded the agenda. "We will speak of control," he told them, "of consistency, quality assurance, and uniformity of conduct. We will have minimum standards and all shall obey them, he warned. We shall have Laws!"

Hammurabi selected his most persnickety eunuchs and sequestered them in a stone hut. There they were to formulate and record the commandments that would bring some sense of sameness to the salad bar of an empire he mastered. They were to draft Hammurabi's Code. The representatives were dismissed to travel back to their posts and await the Law.

While the eunuchs were scribbling and giggling in the stone hut, a trader brought a new work to Hammurabi's attention. "It is called *In Quest of Excellence*, oh great one," he began, "written by two seers named Peters of the Bulky Sweater and Waters the Man. Herein they tell of excellent empires and their traits, and enjoin other tyrants to mime them and find success in so doing, exactly as they do." Hammurabi was enchanted with the work.

He took it everywhere, absorbed in the characteristics of excellent empires. He even took it to the royal zoo, where, sitting on a rock and skimming the work, he lifted his attention to two animated monkeys. Both were sitting on a rock themselves, behind the wooden enclosure, and pretending to be perusing a book of their own. They are mimics, for sure, thought Hammurabi. Then his tyrant brain lit up like a burning olive tree.

"I shall mimic the mimics!" he shouted. "I shall copy what Peters of the Bulky Sweater and Waters the Man have copied. I shall play *monkey see, monkey do*. But with a twist! I'll play *monkey see, monkey do*

*what monkey saw monkey did!"* And he ran to the stone hut and surprised the playful eunuchs and threw the book at them. "Copy the
rules," he demanded, "and make them into my code. Then carve
them in stone and send one copy to every fiefdom, constabulary,
outpost, colony, foothold, and territory I command!"

Before leaving them to their task, Hammurabi made three additional demands. "Make them specific," he told them. "And make them
mandatory. And finally, indicate the punishment for disobedience!"

So the eunuchs got down to work. After they had all the rules
from the imported mime book inscribed, they realized they didn't
tell much. Some were vague, others no more than simple, common
sense. So the eunuchs added specificity and detail, certain
Hammurabi would be delighted. And after thirty days and many
draft tablets, he was. The carved edicts went forth and were erected
in every different land. Well, almost every one.

For the rules were so specific—and many pertained to conditions
found only in Mesopotamia and relied on the Babylonian dialect—
that great difficulty came in interpreting and applying them. Indeed,
the troubles even plagued the tablet carriers.

For example, one such rule was designed to protect the donkey
from harsh mastery, these animals being extremely frail and valuable in Hammurabi's land. Hence, Rule 214 stated, "He who dis-
mounts to drink water while traveling shall first tie his ass to a tree
securely." And on the road to the Hinterlands, three such tablet
bearers came to a desert oasis.

Craving a drink, they proceeded to follow the letter of the law.
Only these men were from the Hinterlands, where the term *ass*
holds an altogether different connotation, and they were aboard
camels. Regrettably, the nearest trees were some thirty paces from
the water's edge, and the men died while straining and pulling
'tween tree and pool. And the camels drank their fill, chortled

heartily, and left. So the tablets never made it to the Hinterlands.

But the remainder of tablets arrived at their destinations, and the people were made to obey them. Let us look at Ethiopia first.

In this East African land, local custom provided for bakers to put aside one loaf in six as alms for the poor. Fresh-baked bread would be placed on a special window ledge where beggars, knowing they were welcome to them, would pass and pluck them away. This benevolence had occurred for generations, and was responsible for peace and tranquility among the disadvantaged. The Law changed this.

For Rule 764 stated, "He who takes what he hasn't bought shall be guilty of theft and lose the offending hand." And though it was contrary to local custom, the governor insisted on strict enforcement. Forty beggars were so mutilated the day after receipt of the tablets, bringing to an end the placing of loaves for the destitute. And thousands of individuals in need, and their families and animals alike, died.

Also, there a custom provided for mass marriages, with all eligible couples so united on the fourth full moon of the year. Ethiopians were romantics, and love was cherished even above the martial arts. Ritual required each groom to pretend to spirit away the heart of his betrothed, abscond to the mountaintop, and await her hand in marriage.

On the first such occasion, just weeks after the tablets arrived, the governor attended the affair. Standing on the local mountain's crest waited two hundred young men, brimming with affection and anticipation as their wives-to-be trekked up to join them in the ceremony of the year.

"Wait!" shouted the governor's lieutenant, "we may be breaking the Law here!" And he cited Rule 765, which read, "Rule 764 is amended to include theft of emotions and affections, as these are larcenies of the heart."

So the ceremony was cancelled, and no weddings were held. And since Rule 653 prohibited man and woman from procreating outside marriage, the Ethiopians began to dwindle in number. The aggravated men then took to the martial arts and began killing more of each other with each passing month. Soon all were dead. The Law must be obeyed. We can only guess which eunuch back in Mesopotamia would have been pleased.

Then there was the Sudan, an urban people with one great and densely populated city on the river. Their problem had been rats, great infestations swimming ashore in the spring and bringing the black death. But generations ago the Sudanese had invented wholly sufficient traps for these vermin and baited them with honey. Thousands of rats would arrive, but by the morning after the invasion, all would be dead.

As the city marshals prepared to bait the traps for the expected infestation this year, they took note of a small inscription in Hammurabi's Code. Rule 1253 declared, "All traps for rodents of all sizes shall be baited with the cheese of goats."

This was puzzling, as the Sudanese did not know of cheese, and neither of goats. Perhaps some eunuch in that stone hut held a goat herd and wished for prosperity. In any case, the Sudanese were overcome, one and all, and the black death leveled them. The rats were pleased. The Law must be obeyed.

Now to the Persians—a thriving sect far distant from Babylon and its Hammurabi, though still among his dominion. Here custom had for hundreds of years dictated a unique deployment. All women between the ages of fifteen and fifty were conscripted as warriors, and great pains were taken by them to defend their border lands against invaders who knew not, nor cared for, Hammurabi. Men, on the other hand, remained at the village, farming and rearing children. The women were bold and fearless, and excellent hunters.

But Rule 8470 read, "All men between the ages of fifteen and fifty shall be warriors and defend the land. Women are forbidden by their natures and this law from taking up arms. They must remain defenseless."

So the Persians tried to adapt. Men were given the slings and bows and arrows. They were horribly inept at handling weapons of war, though, and many accidental woundings and deaths ensued. Then came the Aryans, on horses, with marksmen. As the proficient women watched, their men were annihilated. And in the end, without weaponry or surprise or even concealment, the women were butchered or abducted. Some eunuch in that stone hut held a grievance against women, we suppose. In any case, the Law must be obeyed.

But not everywhere. For the Hinterland, owing to the death in agony of three thirsty camel riders, did not receive the tablets and did not alter local customs and successful operations. They proceeded to work and play and thrive as they knew best, thanks to the fates and the endangered ass rule.

From time to time in this central African province, deep among the rain forests and ringing the ancient crater, came travelers reporting the havoc the tablets were bringing to the world. The Hinterland people cringed at the stories, praying night and day that couriers would never arrive with the Law. And their overlord, a man named DeCent, vowed never to obey them if they should.

Years went by, and DeCent passed away. His son, ComPliant, took over. And a runner from Babylon came and instructed the new leader to report to Hammurabi. Fear flooded the Hinterlands. ComPliant straddled a camel and departed for the reckoning at headquarters. Frightened of his return, the entire population deserted the village and camped along the rim of the crater lake. Each day they would hold hands, five thousand in number, circling the precipice and looking down into the glistening green water. "Give us no Law" they pleaded.

"We know how to manage our affairs best." Hoping these group prayers would assuage their gods, the Hinterland people waited for ComPliant's return.

And return he did, smiling as he eagerly strode up the crater's approach. There the five thousand citizens linked arms and peered first over the edge, then back over their shoulders at ComPliant. A great gasp left their mouths as they each noticed him carrying tablets of stone. Dread crept over them all, and they looked back down into the beautiful emerald depths once more. Then ComPliant harkened to them.

"Have no fear," he shouted. "I do not bring Hammurabi's Law with me!" They began to have hope and to smile, as ComPliant added, "I have, instead, Revision Number One to the Law. And I have more. I have Hammurabi's Strategic Plan, and his Annual Budget!"

At that the five thousand souls—in unison, with arms linked—leapt into the crater and plunged down through the surface of the shimmering pool to their immediate deaths. And the last words ComPliant heard as they fell were, "Let us do what is best for us!"

So the riddle of the bones in the belly of the pit is now put to rest, and the critics of Hammurabi point to his error.

*"Very good," commented the devil, "very good indeed. I especially liked the part about the thirsty travelers tying their asses to a tree!"*

*Prisoner number one blushed. "You said we should amuse you as well as enlighten."*

*"But now enlighten me, Mister control freak. Tell me the lesson. What was Hammurabi's error?"*

*"He tried to determine actions and goals and desires and prefer-*

ences for those he knew not, and he inflicted his particular brand of wisdom upon them. They were codified into catastrophe, ruled into ruin. All in the name of uniformity and consistency, which, absent anything else, seem admirable objectives."

"But nothing is ever 'absent anything else,'" shrieked the devil. "Empires and corporations and institutions do not exist as empty vessels, stupidly waiting for someone from headquarters to fill them. They are viable of their own right, and different. And this is how it should be.

"To impose order where it is needed is just. To do so otherwise is tyranny. To crush the variety of others with stern specificity is the work of eunuchs, not the making of law. And suicide is the only process that works top-down." The prisoner lowered his eyes, waiting to see if the devil was finished. Then came Satan's judgment.

"Congratulations, peon!" Satan snarled.

"For what?"

"You've just become the world's first former eunuch!" He roared with glee and pounded his stone table. The prisoner stood silent, befuddled. "Humor," roared the devil. "Something a control freak wouldn't understand." Then he added this: "For the first time in your career, worm, your fate is totally out of your control. It's in the hands of the eleven imbeciles that follow you. You'd better hope they've learned as much as you have."

Prisoner number one beamed with joy and began to scramble towards the exit. On his way through the gate, he passed the next prisoner, waiting to enter the devil's chamber. "He has a sense of humor," whispered the departing executive through a smile. "Great," sighed the next victim, "I've got a chance!"

"Send in the next idiot!" bellowed the voice of damnation, rustling the curtain with its power. Prisoner number two lost his smile as he was kicked through the gate and onto the brimstone.

# CHAPTER 2

# THOSE AMAZING DIGIT-HEADS
## (A BRIEF HISTORY OF DECISION MAKING)

"And what is lacking cannot be numbered."
**—Ecclesiastes 1:14**

*As the second prisoner stood in the center of the dark chamber, he heard a clattering sound, like dry bones rattling on stone. Then he saw them, two ivory cubes rolling towards him: dice, thrown by the devil.*

*"Not a good way to make decisions, is it?" came the voice from behind the fabric.*

*The prisoner's smile returned, and he took a chance. "It's been tried, your majesty. They call it* divination, *the decision making process of the ancients."*

*"Why in hell would you expect the devil to know about something called* divination?*"*

*"Er, yes, I see what you mean."*

*"Teach me, number cruncher," ordered Satan, "for that is what you are, isn't it? A number cruncher?"*

*"I ran the nation's largest polling service, oh evil one. I ran the numbers up and down, inside and out. I surveyed and weighted and averaged until I could advise corporate leaders what was best, what was safest."*

*"Is that what you call* divination, *then? Doesn't sound too divine to me."*

*"Oh no," replied the prisoner. "The ancients used divination. We use data."*

*"Explain yourself!"*

*"They used omens, sortilege, augury, and spontaneous divination. They threw bones and read goat intestines and followed the ravings of lunatics," explained the petitioner. "They were very primitive."*

*"And what have you modern executives come up with? Something new, something high-tech? Computers, maybe?"*

*"Precisely, sir," replied the prisoner. "Scientifically derived and statistically pure data."*

*"Sounds too good to be true," the devil suggested.*
*The prisoner held up his paper as though it were a legal exhibit. "It is," he answered.*

*"Tell me a story about decisions, then," Satan ordered. "Tell me, Hell's pollster, how executives come to conclusions."*

*"May I take you to a new setting?" inquired prisoner number two. "May we take an island vacation, of sorts?"*

*"By all means!" shouted the devil. "Put in some mystery, and some romance, too. I need a break. I've been stuck down here for what seems like an eternity!"*

*Prisoner number two, always the executive, knew that when the boss laughs, it is wise to laugh along.*

*"Get on with it, fool!" snickered the devil. "Where are you taking me with this story, anyway?"*

*"To Easter Island, sir. To a speck of land lost in the Pacific Ocean. A place teeming with questions."*

*Two more dice spun down the steps, under the curtain, and came to a stop at the prisoner's feet. "Let's roll!" bellowed the boss.*

*Prisoner number two stopped grinning and began his tale.*

They stand sentinel everywhere, these great heads of stone. Identically shaped by an unknown people and huge, they peer outward to the horizon, as if abandoned and longing for their creators. And the visitor looks, too, for clues to the mysterious ones who once populated Easter Island. Were they Polynesian, Peruvian, or from other worlds to which spaceships returned them?

After years of mystery, we now have a theory—and evidence for it. But we must begin with the people's arrival on the mysterious island.

They were refugees from Micronesia, and they came aboard ships of palm fronds lashed together. Once installed on Easter Island, they elected a queen, whose name was Microvision. She reigned for two generations; then the people and she vanished.

They were the Digit-Heads, a decent tribe, and they spent their two generations carving replicas of themselves and burying them neck-deep on the hills and the shores. Each statue was numbered and counted, and each has an open mouth, as if speaking or answering.

There was much to decide at first: whether to stay or depart for other islands, whether to plant edible grasses or tubers, when to send envoys to other lands, and what type of gods to worship. And, as decision-making was new, Microvision tried all the primitive methods: omens, sortilege, augury, and spontaneous divination.

When Microvision saw a mass exodus of sea turtles, for example, she took this as an omen—surely the animals were fleeing because the island would soon erupt like a volcano. Everyone was ordered to follow the turtles to sea, and they did. After two days of faithful, frenzied dogpaddling, they realized that the island was without a volcano, or even a high mountain. Belief in omens ceased.

Then Microvision found a circle of five polished stones on the beach and became fascinated with them. She would roll the stones from her hand and notice strange patterns. She had discovered the practice of sortilege.

While playing this way, she happened to roll all five stones in a straight line, one directly behind the other. Microvision ordered the entire population of several thousand islanders to queue in a similar line. A magic bus would arrive soon, she told them, and they would all be transported to heaven.

So they lined up and waited. Puzzled birds flew by and watched them standing there, perspiring in the sun. Dolphins swam along the shoreline and snickered at them. But no bus passed. "We must not be on the route," offered Microvision, and they dispersed and collapsed.

Two days later they regained their composure, and went back to carving Digit-Head statues. It was infinitely more sensible.

Augury, the next decision making technique, occurred to Microvision through serendipity. She was dining by a forest stream when an overhead hawk lost grasp of its prey. As the queen was lifting a chunk of pineapple to her mouth, a great writhing snake landed on her palm frond plate. "Great gods!" she exclaimed, "it is banded from head to tail!" So thinking this augured well, she commanded the citizens to wrap themselves in ropes, from head to tail.

But loyal as they were, the people balked at this absurd request. "We believe in you," they said, "but we have dogpaddled for days, we have stood in the sun and waited for a bus; but we know we will have difficulty carving Digit-Heads and feeding ourselves and procreating if bound head to tail." Microvision relented. She would have to practice divination of another form.

She called her bursar, one Dipso, from the jungle where he was busy counting coconuts. He had not expected to see her for days, and so was on a binge of fermented milk and quite inebriated. He was drinking and dancing and frolicking with girls, a practice called "bungle in the jungle" and could not right himself before his audience with Microvision.

So when he wobbled to her hut and she asked him to assist her with decisions, Dipso went into song and dance—too far gone to appreciate the sobriety of the circumstance. Not having seen this aspect of Dipso, Microvision seized on it as spontaneous divination. "Tell us, oh Dipso," she implored, "what shall the Digit-Heads be doing to please the gods?"

"Let's bungle in the jungle!" slurred Dipso, grinning and swaying like a wind-blown palm. Microvision seized her conch horn and blew a roaring note across the land. "To the jungle!" she shouted, "where we will perform the bungle!" She had no idea what this signified, but was pleased to see her subjects take to it so avidly. Perhaps Dipso had a special line to the gods after all.

Hammers were dropped all over the island in the rush to comply with the queen's wishes. All carving stopped, and several people were injured in the clamor and rush to the dancing and drinking orgy. But after three days and three nights, Microvision tired of watching so much unrestricted joy and revelry. Besides, not one man had asked her to bungle. "Back to the Digit-Heads," she commanded. "The party is over!" Then to her diviner Dipso she remarked, "Go lie on the beach, man, and dry yourself out."

Then Microvision went to the beach herself, to stroll and think of new ways to decide on important issues. There she happened upon her niece, a solitary girl, sometimes quite foolish. She was counting the grains of sand and was well into seven digits at that point. But she had an idea, this niece, so she stopped her counting and spoke with Microvision.

"What you need, old woman" she began, "is a management information system." The queen stared at her in puzzlement, and the girl went on. "A management information system, your highness, or better yet, a decision-support system. It will tell you exactly what must be done. Gather your data, survey your people, compile the results, then act accordingly." And she explained everything to the queen, who eagerly accepted it, and went on to design and construct such a system immediately.

Thus, the Digit-Heads became the most polled, surveyed, sampled, and analyzed people in the Pacific. Forms were contrived, listing alternatives, and pollsters circulated them to all citizens. The data were sanitized, unwarranted answers were discarded, and curves plotted. The decision support machine cranked and spun its way through the most perplexing issues. And Microvision, like so many executives to follow, sighed with relief. Here was the answer to her prayers. Now, relieved of the burden of decisions, she could enjoy the perquisites of power with none of the responsibility. With a clear conscience and the righteousness of one who could never be faulted, she simply acted by the dictates of the digits.

One of her early polls was taken to determine the need for more statues, there being only ten at the time. The question was, "Which would you prefer?" and the possible responses were: "(1) To carve another Digit-Head from stone, (2) to be drowned in the lagoon, or

(3) to marry Microvision." The results were astonishing! Ninety-nine percent of respondents favored carving more statues. So more were ordered. Six males who chose alternatives two or three were seen slipping from the beach at midnight, paddling furiously on a reed canoe.

Another poll asked, "What do we need the most?" and the possible responses were: "(1) More statues, (2) the sacrifice of an honest woman, or (3) another turtle emigration." And behold! Ninety-five percent of the citizens chose more statues! Twenty women were seen paddling off in a hastily constructed ship the next evening. Microvision wasn't concerned: Ten were virtuous, and ten had weak legs. Besides, they weren't statistically relevant. More people were ordered to take up hammer and chisel.

Then a third survey. Questions included: "Given a choice, would you rather (1) take a bus to heaven, or (2) keep pounding and chipping." And 59 percent went for the chisels and hammers. "Majority rules," shouted Micronesia. "This is fun!" But the chipping went slowly now, for two hundred men and women and children were standing in a line in the sun. In three days they perished from exposure.

Noticing this, Microvision toyed with the next poll, determined to test the stamina of her statue carving citizens for good. She gathered the remaining chippers in front of her hut. There they stood, arms drooping at their sides, stone chips embedded in their skin, dust coating their eyes. All were apprehensive, but all were too tired of pounding stones to care much.

Dipso, with his bloodshot eyes and shaking hands, had been granted special dispensation from rock chipping. In fine spirits, he had been drinking fermented coconut milk for twelve days straight, and lurched to his favored spot next to the queen with a mighty belch. Then he scanned the crowd, leering at the young women among them.

"We shall have a contest," Microvision announced, "to determine your carving ability." Then she explained the rules. "My assistants shall keep assiduous count of the quantity of rock each of you removes. The person with the least stone to his or her credit shall be bound like a snake and tossed into the lagoon. The person with the most stone shall be wed to Dipso. The remainder of you shall dogpaddle in the sea for as long as it takes for Dipso and his new spouse to consummate their marriage. Now, my children, that should motivate you! Take up your hammers!"

Microvision retreated to her hut to await the outcome, with Dipso, smiling, at her side. When the night came, Dipso was rejected from the hut for his stench and gross manners. But as the queen lay in her bed and Dipso sprawled in the weeds outside, they heard no hammering in the distance, for none was being done. The people, instead, were weaving escape vessels. In the morning, all were gone.

Surprised, the queen arose and waddled to the low hills. They were empty, save for the silent sentinels and the tall grass waving like the sea. Tools were hastily abandoned around unfinished monuments, with Digit-Heads left half-formed. And up staggered Dipso, eyes red and face puffy—and scratching himself.

"They have left me," cried Microvision, "and we have now a population of two. It is not a statistically significant sample," she fretted, "and I cannot decide what to do!" And in her anger she picked up a hammer at her feet and threw it against a nearby Digit-Head, sending a tiny sliver of stone from its face.

"Behold the contest winner," shouted Dipso, slobbering on his chest and advancing toward the queen. "And behold my new bride!"

We do not know how they perished, these final two inhabitants of Easter Island. We can only speculate. Perhaps they did wed, but consumption of fermented coconut milk on a continuous basis has been known to inhibit virility. Perhaps this explains the death of the race.

Or maybe it is the statistically proven limit of dogpaddling, which has been demonstrated to fail after prolonged periods of time, even for a queen. And to our knowledge, there are no buses stopping on Easter Island, to heaven or otherwise.

We simply have no data.

*"No data?" asked the voice from the dark throne. It was the first time he'd spoken during the entire reading. "Perhaps that is the answer," he snorted. "Don't you see, numbskull?"*

*Prisoner number two began to calculate the probability of his ascending to earth again, of saving himself and his colleagues from an eternity in the inferno. The numbers weren't comforting. While he continued to figure silently, Satan answered his own question.*

*"The Digit-Heads had all the data in the world, and it was immediately available to their decision maker. Yet the result was thousands of stupid statues, a disappearing population, and a finale too disgusting for even me to imagine."*

*"Hell," the devil continued, "the drunkard with his* spontaneous divination *shtick had more sense than Microvision and all the modern executives who follow in her stupid footsteps. Any leader who expects to escape decisions by relying solely on data is no better than Dipso! Management by the numbers is no better than bungle in the jungle," he snarled through his teeth. "And a hell of a lot less fun."*

*"Beautifully said," the prisoner told him. "What a wise leader you must be."*

*"Don't press your luck, number cruncher. I may not be wise, but I can spot a brownnoser from a mile away!"*

*Prisoner number two was dismissed and ordered to send in the next executive. As he scurried toward the exit on cat's feet, he overheard the devil calling to his assistant. "Bring me a flagon of fermented coconut milk. And some dancing girls. Now!"*

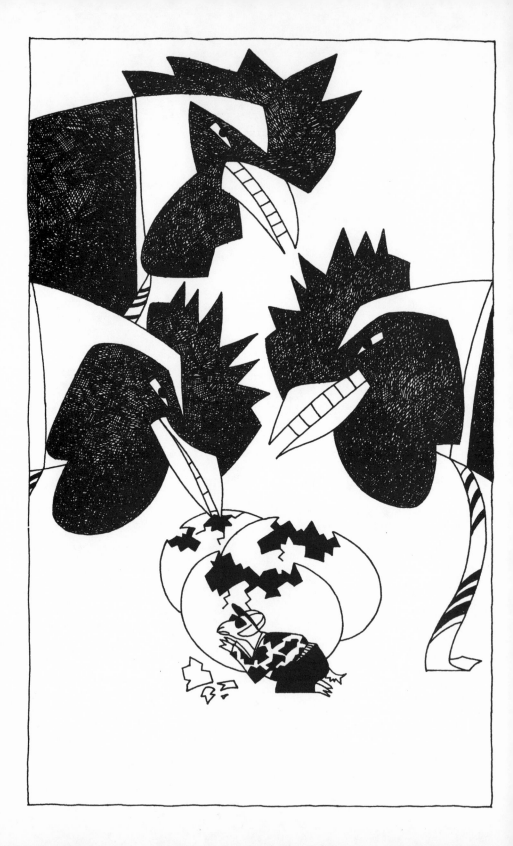

# THE GOLDEN EGG CAFE
## (HOW COMPROMISE CHOKES INNOVATION)

"Of all sad words of tongue or pen,
The saddest are these: It might have been!"

**—John Greenleaf Whittier,** "The Saddest Words"

*When prisoner number three was first manacled to her blistering steel desk, the short note scrawled at the top of her yellow legal pad flayed her conscience like a cat o' nine tails. It had been almost a decade, yet the memory and the pain were still there. This prisoner had been the chief executive officer of a giant food conglomerate.*

*She made her name and her career from shaving not ounces, but grams off fast food portions. She sliced seconds from cooking times, spreading quality as thinly as mayonnaise on a sesame seed bun. Prisoner number three squeezed profits from food service operations as if the company were one giant plastic ketchup bottle. If she had been a bartender, she'd have been justly accused of watering down the bourbon. Instead, she formulated fillers, extenders, and packaging that made what was cheap and fast look wholesome and rich.*

*She had buried this particular project, tucked it way back in corporate records. She had hoped it would be forgotten. If no one ever mentioned the name, ever, so much the better. But there it was, scrawled atop her writing pad. The devil's assistant knew how to hurt, how to reopen old wounds. At the top of her pad, prisoner number three read, "The Golden Egg Cafe."*

*While the fast food magnate stood in front of the evil judge's throne, she felt his eyes on her through the curtain. That old familiar sensation, she realized, even here—in Hell. But she was used to standing out, used to their surprise and their suspicion. In his first remark, Satan confirmed both.*

*"I thought you were all men?" the devil inquired.*

*"So did they," she told him. "So does everyone."*

*Then something totally unexpected happened. All of a sudden, from out of nowhere, rose a sickening belch. And, more surprisingly, a cardboard bucket was lofted into the air, cleared the curtain, bounced along the brimstone, and rested at her feet. The devil had been eating take-out chicken.*

*The prisoner was so shocked, she spoke without thinking. "I didn't know they deliver here," she sighed in amazement.*

*"They have a hell of a market penetration," replied a deep voice from behind the curtain. "They'll do anything for a dollar."*

*Prisoner number three was silent, waiting for her sentence without even reading her story, knowing for certain that her sins were unforgivable. But then Satan seemed to be moving. The curtain shimmered with a rustling sound, and a hand appeared under it.*

*The prisoner expected the devil to have scaly, amphibious skin, or at least claws of iron or blood-soaked bone. Yet the hand was almost human. A little burned, but that was to be expected. What wasn't expected was what it was clutching. A chicken bone—a wishbone.*

*"Go on," urged the devil, wiggling the bone to get the prisoner's attention. "Pull it. Take a chance!"*

*The prisoner froze in fear, anchored to the stone, motionless and silent. The devil laughed.*

*"That's it, isn't it?"*

*"What is, your crispy one?"*

*"That's your fatal trait, fast-food fortune maker. You are unwilling to take any kind of risk."*

*"I don't like games, your heinous highness. I prefer to know the*

*outcome, and predictable results are more manageable."*

*"I know, I know. And that is why the chicken bone is an apt test for you. For we have a saying here in Hell. We say that a great idea is never killed in one stroke. Instead, it dies a slow and neglected death. Innovation is never executed—it is pecked to death by chickens.*

*"Have you heard of reckless prudence?" asked the grand inquisitor.*

*"No, sir. It sounds like an oxymoron. How can prudence be reckless?"*

*"Did you forget about the Golden Egg Cafe, coward? Did you learn nothing these past two weeks?"*

*"Yes, sir; I mean, no, sir . . . I mean . . . "*

*"Innovation is the issue here!" said the devil, "not equivocation!"*

*"Shall I read my story, then?"*

*"By all means," answered the devil, "for once in your miserable life—go for it!"*

*"I must first explain that the historic events leading to this story are factual. There was a mysterious CIA, a gold rush, a trend toward natural foods. And, of course, there were chickens. Thousands of them."*

*"Cut the caveats and disclaimers, woman! Tell the story!"*

he CIA set this drama in motion when it decided to train Tibetan soldiers. "The Company" was hoping for rebellion against the Communist Chinese from these mountain people, and invited separatist leaders to send troops to the United States for training. But the affair had to remain secret. The enemy couldn't discover that the United States was training rebels to attack, the enemy here being two: the Chinese and the American public. A mountain hideout was necessary.

One was found in an abandoned army camp high in the

Colorado mountains. Cargo planes loaded with culture-shocked Tibetan mountain men landed at Petersen Field, an Air Force base near Colorado Springs. Buses with windows taped against detection were snuck into the field and loaded. The trip, and this story, began at night.

They headed west, and up, into the mountains. Jeeps and supply trucks originating at nearby Fort Carson joined the convoy, their headlights slit and their American soldiers wondering what in the hell was going on.

Up into the thin air they climbed, this clandestine coupling. Staying off the main routes, they crept along narrow ledges and passed small, forgotten towns clinging to the edges of the Rocky Mountains. With windows fogged, the travelers pulled their field jackets on. It was getting colder, and darker, and quieter.

They rumbled slowly through the national forests, up through Buena Vista, past Granite, Leadville, then Stringtown and Red Cliff. The air and the inhabitants were thinning with each mile. The convoy turned off onto a dirt road and entered Camp Hale, secret site of mountain training. Secret since World War II. This night, it would come alive again.

As military policemen waved the trucks and buses through a cattle gate, Private First Class Billy Goetz shook himself awake. He had been a soldier for six months, and he knew how to doze when he could. He was guarding the field mess. Billy was a cook. Late of Pueblo, and his Army buddies called him a mongrel.

That's because Billy had an Anglo father and a Hispanic mother. He had a tenth grade education and nothing, absolutely nothing else. When he was drafted he got his first pair of boots, his first dental exam, his first new underwear—right out of the box. Now he was getting his first look at people from the other side of the world. The mongrel checking out the Mongols. The descendants of

Genghis Khan facing the descendent of Hernando Cortez, in the frigid air of the mined-out mountains. Jesus, it was cold!

The Tibetans were hungry, so Billy got to work. By the time that first breakfast was completed, Billy discovered many things about these strange men. They wore Mickey Mouse hats with big floppy earflaps, and they sported huge drooping moustaches. And they didn't like Army food. They grunted a lot and spat the army chow he'd cooked onto the flat ground surrounded by high mountains.

Camp Hale is isolated, totally. Radio signals can't get in. Humans don't want to. With mountains on four sides, it was a perfect hide-away. The training began, and Billy experimented with the rations, trying to please the gruff GIs from the Himalayas. It was tough.

But as the weeks went by, he picked up some of their language, and interpreters arrived. And one food they would eat was easy to fix: eggs. He boiled them, scrambled them, fried them, and made them like no Army manual ever specified. Finally, he made them like his momma did, and the Tibetans ate them that way—and no other.

They called it "bird in a nest," but to Billy it was just a fried egg placed in the center of a piece of bread. Poke out a hole, dump in the egg, let it fry. Flip it, slip it to 'em, and watch 'em smile.

Then they told him of special butters they used, butter from goats and cows raised on the range in Tibet, in the cool, clean clouds. And they spoke of the chickens they raised, and the feeds they would allow and those they wouldn't. Billy emulated the recipe to the extent his supplies allowed. They said it was okay, but they'd had better.

In four months the Tibetans were back on the papered-over buses and rolling down to the airport again. While they had been rappelling and hiking and camping in the Rocky Mountain winter-time, some bureaucrat in Washington got cold feet. The deal was off. Billy said good-bye, finished off his time, and drifted back to

Pueblo in his army shoes.

Hitching out the south gate of Fort Carson, he made it a few miles to Fountain, population 4,000. There he got drunk and spent his separation money at a dive called the Roundup Saloon. He worked there washing dishes for two days, getting up bus fare to Pueblo. Then the cook fell sick, and Billy hit the grill. He never made it to Pueblo. He stayed at the Roundup, lassoed to a short order job, for twenty-four years.

Then came his golden age. South African gold was up because the British were down—in the Falklands, fighting Argentina. A mini-boom hit Colorado and several other mined-out states. Billy met a man on the way to Leadville, just outside Camp Hale. He had some money, he wanted to open a restaurant for the miners, and he needed Billy. Billy threw his spatula into a grease pit and took off.

There he found his element. Hungry miners and a short order cook who does eggs are an explosive combination, in any time. He opened the Golden Egg Cafe, selling beer and birds in a nest, and they knocked the doors off the hinges. Leadville was hot, precious metals were the reason, and Billy Goat, as they called him, had his own gold mine.

But as things happen, the boom was short lived, and after a year or so the only ones sitting at Billy's tables were the occasional elk hunters, hippies on a Rocky Mountain high, and tourists and journalists straying over from hip spots like Telluride or Aspen. Leadville was not on their maps. Billy Goat was left high and dry. And near broke.

Truckers kept him alive, stone haulers and the ones ferrying corn and barley to the Coors brewery over in Golden. To cut costs, Billy started raising yard chickens and getting his butter from a weird group of natural ranchers on the high plain, up near the divide. They were raising cattle without hormones or antibiotics,

42

letting them feed on the range, selling the products for a premium to a health conscious market back East. The butter was okay, for range-fed beef cows, but the Army sure wouldn't have approved.

One afternoon, Billy was out slinging corn at his chickens in the gravel lot when a trucker screeched his air brakes and slid into his life. The guy wanted a beer. They got to talking.

"What's that crap leaking out the back of yer trailer?" Billy asked.

"That's mash, I suppose. Just picked up a load at Coors. It's the leftovers from making beer."

"Sure is messing up my lot," Billy said.

"Yeah," sighed the drinker, "but look at them chickens, will ya? They's goin after it big!"

And they were. Fighting over it, pecking the feathers off each other in their attempts to get as much of the slop as they could.

"Reckon you could stop by here often?" Billy asked the trucker.

"How 'bout once a week?"

"Sounds good."

It was good, for the chickens got free feed and Billy's costs went down another notch or two. Then the reporter came by.

He'd seen her type before, all decked out in hiking boots, down vests, and Lands' End nylon packs. She'd been doing a lifestyle piece over in Telluride. She wanted some local color, and strayed across into Leadville. And she couldn't wait to get out. But she was hungry, and Denver was hours away. She got a bird in a nest. Mash-fed chickens and skinny, grass-eating cattle, and she loved it.

"This is totally awesome!" she told Billy, as he was handing her the check. "Like, where did you learn to cook like that?"

Billy thought of telling her the Army, or the Roundup Saloon, but neither sounded impressive enough. So he scratched his scraggly goatee and replied, "From Tibet, a long time ago."

"Holy Karma!" she exclaimed, "Tibet? The holy land, the pure place, the Lost Horizon, the 120-year-old-lifespan Tibet?"

"Land o' Mongols butter does it," he crowed, enjoying this, "and chickens with a buzz on helps."

Her piece went out over a modem from Denver that night. In two weeks Telluride came to Leadville, to the Golden Egg Cafe. Billy Goat was *in*! Everybody loved this bird in a nest, and the lore behind it. People with a nature thing, people with an anti-fat thing, people with a longevity thing, people with an anti-communist thing or a religious thing, and people with money and influence. And it didn't take long before people with legal things showed up.

They cut a quick deal. Billy Goat was to be president, the franchises would spread coast to coast, the money would pile up higher than Pike's Peak! Forget Colonel Sanders, they screamed, we've got Private Billy! Forget about Big Macs, they swore, we've got SOS: shit-on-a-shingle!

Billy insisted on two things: He would use the name "Billy Goat from Leadville," and he would control the recipe. You're the boss, they told him. You're the goose that lays the golden eggs! Then they all laughed, lit cigars, and started talking about Billy Goat T-shirts and action dolls and getting the Dahli Lama for thirty-second TV spots.

Then before you know it, Billy was on the phone to his agent in Chicago. There was a problem with the name, "Billy Goat from Leadville."

"You ever watch *Saturday Night Live* reruns?" he asked Billy.

"Once in a while. Why?"

"Ever see the skits where Belushi and Akroyd are in the hamburger joint and the cooks keep saying, 'cheeseburger, cheeseburger, no fries—chips, no Coke—Pepsi'?"

"Yeah, that was hilarious. So what?"

"So, they based it on a cafe here in Chicago, a real cafe. The place is called The Billy Goat. We don't need litigation, my friend, not at this stage. We don't want to scare away investors, do we? No way, Jose."

Billy guessed not. Then came the marketing report. Leadville was a handicap, it turned out, a definite no-no. "At a time when people are phobic of lead—lead in paint, lead in gasoline, lead in the water pipes—we couldn't sell Leadville to people on death row, much less an upwardly mobile, health conscious consumer."

So they called it "Private Billy's Golden Egg Cafe" and made the workers wear Gomer Pyle suits and told Billy to stop wearing his brand new, bonus-bought snakeskin boots. He'd have to appear in Army shoes—that was the image they wanted. That was how they wanted to "position" him. So Billy tied on those cheap, cardboard-thin, prison-issue low quarters and began to wish he was back in Camp Hale again.

Then they had trouble getting the timing down. Food had to be made in an average of thirteen seconds from order placement to customer delivery to make the economics work out. The teenagers in Gomer Pyle suits were trying their little Billy-loving hearts out, but couldn't average better than twenty seconds per bird in a nest. An executive meeting was held.

"I like your tie," said a Madison Avenue type as Billy entered the conference room. "It looks like it was extruded!" Everyone laughed, trying to relieve the tension. Then an industrial engineer raised his hand and said, "That's it! We can extrude the stuff!"

So the process specialist took a night flight to Charlotte, North Carolina, to the factory where plastic PVC drainage pipe was extruded, and came back with a deal that made the food experts grin. "We rent a thousand-foot line, convert it from making PVC to producing birds in a nest, see. Then we fill the hoppers with egg yolks, whites, and flour. We have a pipe within a pipe within a pipe. Pipe one pulls yellow, pipe two white, and pipe three batter for the nest. Our guys tell me we can extrude forty feet a minute! The stuff goes through hot water and then cold water and congeals in an infinitely long tube!

Then he brought out a loaf of the stuff, a great wobbly gelatinous tube and let it slither on the table. Pulling a knife from his briefcase he sliced a half-inch thick disk from the end. "Voila!" he exclaimed, "endless bird in a nest! And check out the consistency! Each slice exactly like the others." Then Billy remembered the Tibetans marveling at his real version, claiming the golden center surrounded by the tan corona made them think of Tibetan sunsets—each one the same, but every one different.

So they took an option on the line. The stuff got sticky, so they added a kaolin hopper, then injected wood resin for consistency, and crushed limestone for filler and to get the women/calcium market.

"The beer link is deadly," claimed one woman, reporting on the test market results. "At a time when we've got declining alcohol sales, everybody-who's-anybody against drunken driving, and warning labels on every six pack, can we really tout a good that relies on inebriated chickens?"

Who could argue with her? They started feeding the birds pellets of something or another.

Then they found the Japanese fed their chickens fish meal, and switched to that. It made the eggs taste like carp, and the yolks went near white. But none of them cared—it was cheaper. Besides, the Japanese did it, so it had to be brilliant.

When they found that the ranchers who produced the drug-free range beef could only supply one-tenth the butter they needed, they switched to substitutes. First margarine, then hydrogenated vegetable oil, then frozen palm oil because it had a lower flash point and a higher viscosity—key manufacturing characteristics. It also lubricated the extrusion process, and that alone would've done it.

Billy stood and watched all this, powerless to stop it. Sure, he'd complain that each modification was ruining the original idea, but they ignored him. "You're the golden goose," they'd tell him, "but we're the extrusion experts," or "we're the viscosity experts," or the time-and-motion experts, or extender experts, or lifestyle analysts.

Before long Billy lost track of exactly what it was they were going to make and sell. A simple egg in a piece of toast turned into an imitation PVC, hydrogenated, carp-smelling, viscous, low flash point, quality-controlled, teenaged-sliced tube of gelatinous extrusion. And he sat in conference rooms with his feet in Army shoes under the table: the goose that extruded the infinitely long, continuous, consistent tube of goo.

The first restaurant opened with great fanfare and megabucks in promotion. They couldn't get the Dahli Lama for their ad spots, of course, so they settled for a guy who once played a Sherpa guide on an American Express commercial. He was actually from Pueblo—Billy knew him in high school.

And when it was all over, the guy who wasn't a Tibetan but played one on TV made more out of the deal than Billy Goetz. He had an agent. He got his money up front. Billy was on contingency. Except for what he spent on the snakeskin boots they wouldn't let him wear, he didn't get a cent. Seems the American public couldn't get into cold, quivering, pale, rubbery, frisbee-like dollops of fish goo on a sesame seed bun.

The mongrel feeling came back to Billy as he thumbed a ride down from Leadville to the base of the mountains. He didn't have a dime, and it was raining on his army shoes. He got a ride to the fountain of his youth, and stood outside the Roundup for a few moments, wondering if he should go inside. He was thinking of the

CIA, the papered buses, the strong but strange men from the mountains, the gold rush, the truck from Golden, the golden goose, the greasy goo.

Then the screen door slammed behind the would-be innovator, the poor boy willing to risk everything, used and discarded by the rich men willing to risk nothing. Billy sauntered into the darkness and the din, and disappeared. Rounded up. Gobbled up. Pecked to death by chickens.

*Prisoner number three finished reading, took her eyes off the pad, and looked around the dingy cavern. The devil was silent, or perhaps he'd left midway through the story. Characteristically, prisoner number three began to worry.*

*Then she spotted a motion out of the corner of her eye. Something was moving under the curtain. A wishbone again. The devil was wiggling it suggestively, offering another chance. The prisoner decided to go for it.*

*She fought back her fear as she approached the bone, smelling the breath of the devil himself. It gave off the heat and stench of diesel exhaust. But the prisoner bolstered her meager courage and lowered herself to her knees and, in a flash, grabbed the greasy bone and pulled it with all her might. It snapped away.*

*"Did you win or lose?" inquired the unseen demon.*

*"I don't know. I can't remember, your highness, whether the one who has the long segment or the short segment loses."*

*"Neither!"*

*"What?"*

*"It doesn't matter whether you have the long end or the short*

*end, stupid! The loser is the one who never pulls the bone!"*

*"You mean, the one who plays it safe?" asked prisoner number three, beginning to make the connection between the story and the devil's wishbone game.*

*"Reckless prudence," replied the devil. "The most dangerous position is taking no position. In business, the biggest risk is taking no risk at all."*

*"Is that the lesson of innovation?" asked the prisoner.*

*"Just look around you," Satan said. "What do you see?"*

*"Fire," answered the executive, "and steam and smoke. And I smell foul air and hear screams of pain and anguish."*

*"It is a scene unending and unchanged. It is never new, never better. Everything you see here was described by Milton or Dante centuries ago. We have no innovation in Hell."*

*Prisoner number three listened, and considered. Satan continued.*

*"We have no innovation in Hell because we have no innovators. You will not find the likes of Billy Goetz here."*

*"No innovators? Why is that?"*

*"Because they have spent their time in Hell on earth! Trying to improve! Trying to take chances! Trying to get cowards like you to risk!"*

*The prisoner winced and began to panic. "Does that mean I lose? Does that mean I won't escape from Management Hell?"*

*"You're outta here, woman," came the verdict from behind the curtain, "faster than an Egg McMuffin. The story had nothing to do with it. It was the wishbone test. You tried. Therefore, you win. Now go," commanded the devil, "and by the way."*

*"Yes sir?"*

*"Tell my assistant to send in some cole slaw—and some napkins. I've got grease all over my fingers!"*

# CALIGULA'S CHARIOT RACE
## (QUALITY CHALLENGES A CHEAT)

"Competition, which is the instinct of selfishness,
is another word for dissipation of energy,
while combination is the secret of efficient production."
—**Edward Bellamy**, *Looking Backward*

*Reflecto was escorting the fourth prisoner through a narrow cavern on the way to his appointment with Satan when three agitated acolytes rushed up to him and blocked his path.*

*"The magma lakes are perilously low!" one exclaimed. "The pumps are worn, and the sinners who man them are dropping like flies!"*

*"Put more workers on them," Reflecto suggested, "and use the whips!"*

*"But they're working overtime as it is!"*

*"Put on a graveyard shift. Take some sinners from the bellows force, and man it with a skeleton crew," Reflecto told him, knowing full well the stopgap measures wouldn't solve the problem for long. Then he muttered to the prisoner, "We're operating this business on a shoestring. The old man is tight as hell!"*

*A second assistant was waving a computer printout, his face red and creased with worry. "Report from the field reps," he began, having cornered his superior in the tunnel. "Funds are running out up there, and they threaten a strike!"*

*Reflecto forced a smile. "Those temptation teams can really run up an expense account!"*

"Inflation," exclaimed the assistant. "Greed is harder to feed these days."

"Tell them to focus on sex or sloth this month," Reflecto countered, "or gluttony. Tell them to quit trying to compete with Wall Street. Those guys are out of our league!"

The third reporter held up a series of blueprints. "Steam piping is deteriorating," he told Reflecto, waving the drawings as evidence. "We need to replace faulty valves soon."

"It's not in the capital budget," Reflecto answered. "Satan has us on an austerity plan, fool. Let them leak for another week."

When the three disgruntled demons scurried away, Reflecto turned to his prisoner. "See what I have to put up with?" he asked. "I'm tired of it all! Satan is so cheap! He screws our suppliers, shafts our subcontractors, shortchanges our field reps." Then he held his hand to his mouth and whispered. "Don't let this get out, but I'm looking around. My resume is on the street."

As he was finishing this last comment, a steam fitting running the length of the corridor erupted and shot a blast of superheated fluid into his side. Reflecto jumped and howled, rubbing his forearm in pain. The steam had found a small tear in his sleeve, scalding his arm before he could leap out of its path.

"Damned cheap suits!" he exclaimed. "Look at this fabric, will ya? The old man insists on buying from the low bidder!"

Prisoner number four remained silent, though he understood Reflecto's frustration and empathized with his predicament. He had seen it before. Hell, he'd lived it. When he finally met the devil, he'd tell the old skinflint all about it.

"The subject of your story?" Satan asked, impatient at the delay in bringing the prisoner to him.

"Ancient Rome," the prisoner responded. "Cost control, vendor management, quality."

*"Sounds boring. I know all about those."*

*"How about if I spice it up with a little greed, gluttony, deceit, theft, perversion, murder, duplicity? Maybe even throw in some gore and ghosts?"*

*"Now you've got my attention!" Satan squealed, unable to contain his glee. "Sounds like a game show in Hell!"*

*"Close, your putrescence. Actually, it's ancient Rome. But the graphic details continue to this day, up there, in my world of business."*

*"Let the games begin," shouted the devil. "And don't spare the gratuitous violence!"*

aius Caligula was certainly insane. He believed he was a god, and to prove it he practiced incest with his three sisters, claiming Jupiter had done so with his very sister, Juno. But as evil and degenerate as he was, the man was a bona fide celebrity. The secret to Caligula's popularity among citizens of Rome was that, as emperor, he amused them. Caligula was the original party animal.

He lavished money on the masses, and nothing stood in the way of the great gladiatorial contests he held in the coliseum for their entertainment. When told of the high price of raw meat for his circus animals, for example, he ordered that petty criminals be used instead. He lined up a row of accused and commanded his soldiers, "Kill every man between that bald head and the one over there." They obeyed.

One day Caligula was presiding over a sacrifice at the temple. He was to ceremoniously strike a beast with a wooden hammer. On a whim, Caligula turned to the priest holding the animal and swung the mallet at his skull, knocking him unconscious. Caligula considered this a hilarity. And, of course, the remaining priests broke out in a chorus of nervous laughter. Being priest to Caligula was a precarious position.

Being invited to one of his banquets was also a dubious honor. At one such feast, Caligula began to laugh to himself. When a courtesan asked the source of his mirth, Caligula announced "It just occurred to me that I only have to give one nod and your throats will be cut." Thereupon the merriment was quite subdued.

But for all his faults, Caligula knew how to throw one hell of a chariot race, the greatest of which was to occur in celebration of the birth of his sixth son. For the emperor's concubine (and sister) was with child and expected to issue a male, or be slain. Suffice it to say, stress was rampant at the time.

One of Caligula's former generals, Edsel, had command of the imperial chariot works. Hired by Caligula to supply all the Roman legions, Edsel had amassed a fortune crafting thousands of chariots of similar design and usefulness. Edsel shared Caligula's perverse sense of grandeur and taste, and hence fashioned great, garish chariots requiring teams of strong horses to pull them.

Edsel's official chariots were also notable for their unreliability, many failing in the midst of battle and plunging their riders to their deaths. But Caligula favored their ornamentation, their false fronts and ostentatious wheels, and ordered more to be made. Edsel thrived.

To extract maximum profit from each such chariot, Edsel brandished great bargaining clout among wheelwrights, coopers, carpenters, and harness workers. With such large orders, he threatened each supplier and had them bid against one another for his favor. Lower the price, he would tell them, or forget the work. And when one supplier would agree to such paltry terms, Edsel's procurers would turn to the next and say, "We have a price. But you must be lower than it." In this fashion, the suppliers through the empire compromised their products and undercut each other to such an extent that they were afraid to ride in the finished chariots.

To avoid penury, the wheelwrights substituted softer brass for iron on the wheel rims. The harness workers used skins of stray dogs and cats instead of fine calves. Carpenters began to omit one nail in three, and to pray that Edsel's procurers would not notice the absence. The deception spread.

Even the smiths who were paid to shod the imperial horses took to painting their hooves with a mixture of mercury and lampblack, giving the false impression that they had shoes of iron. So occupied were Edsel's procurers with price, they suspected nothing. The few who noticed were ambivalent. "Who cares?" they would ask themselves. "The riders will be killed before the horses even lather."

When Caligula was considering the upcoming race, an ally rode into Rome at the head of a small detail of soldiers. A messenger brought the event to Caligula, who strode into the square and was immediately taken by the stranger's chariot. It was different from those built by Edsel, smaller and of subdued design.

"Who built this alien vehicle?" Caligula asked. And the stranger replied, "This is the work of a freed slave from Gaul. A man who builds only a small number and caters to the centurion trade. For centurions know a chariot must be strong and dependable, or they will suffer in battle."

Caligula looked the wagon over again and scoffed. "Have this maker brought to Rome," he ordered, "and race his finest against Edsel! We shall see who Jupiter will favor!"

So it was done. The freed slave, Technicus, arrived with his trusted suppliers and craftsmen. For where Edsel had opened his bidding to hundreds of suppliers, Technicus was more selective, hiring only the best and giving them assurance of continual employ.

Whereas Edsel lived by the motto, "Expect the minimum price

from the maximum bidders," when dealing with procured materials and services, Technicus reversed this philosophy, proclaiming, "Expect the maximum quality from the minimum partners." For Technicus looked on his suppliers as partners; he even dined with them and shared knowledge among them. Edsel, on the other hand, scorned and cheated his furnishers.

As the day for the race approached and both builders worked on their chariots, Caligula began to have disturbing dreams. In one, he saw the great god Jupiter before him. And Jupiter said to Caligula, "The leagues shall be the legacy." This left Caligula puzzled, and he consulted a trembling oracle the very next morning.

"It is forthright," the oracle explained. "By leagues, Jupiter means the distance for the great chariot race. And by legacy, he indicates the number of sons you shall have on that day."

So Caligula, knowing the meaning, changed the distance for the race. Where five leagues was traditional, he proclaimed that the length in leagues would equal the number of sons he had fathered. And the citizens, knowing of the expectant birth, began betting on the outcome of a six-league contest. Caligula, so sure of victory, wagered huge fleets and distant lands on the event.

Edsel was ecstatic. "I know my chariot will travel six leagues," he attested, "for I have seen it done once." Then he instructed his liverymen to extend the life of the chariot with minor additions. "Six leagues is all I need," he said, "and not one more!"

Technicus was indifferent, however. For Technicus had ridden his chariots for hundreds of leagues without incident. One more league would not affect the outcome.

On the morning of the great day, as crowds of plebeians and patricians poured into the coliseum, Caligula proclaimed that the victor would be granted a contract to supply five thousand chariots to the imperial army.

56

Then Edsel himself rode his majestic chariot onto the field. It was all festooned with fish fins and eagle effigies and dog skin harnesses, and the crowd stood and cheered. Technicus then made his entrance, upon a sleek and simple and sound machine, and the crowd drew its breath.

Just at that moment, a messenger ran up to Caligula with glad tidings, for it seemed that Caligula's concubine had just delivered twins! And both males! Remembering the epiphany of Jupiter and the counsel of the oracle, Caligula commanded the race distance to be increased to seven leagues!

Edsel and Technicus then drew their chariots to the starting line, and Caligula made his way to the great gong, which he was to strike to begin the event. As the emperor held the mallet high in the air, Edsel saluted him by striking his breast with his fist. And Caligula, true to habit, struck not the gong but the head of the official starter, who fell to his knees. At this prearranged signal, Edsel lashed his team and thundered off. Technicus, caught by surprise, followed at a distance of one-half a league.

With the crowd cheering and drinking and raising its arms in a tidal wave of motion, Edsel maintained his lead through four leagues. Dust rose from the arena as the chariots spun around each turn.

Then Edsel's lead animal broke its dog skin yoke and ran from the team, and Edsel slowed somewhat. Technicus gained. Edsel's left wheel threw three spokes into the crowd, impaling a wine vendor and agitating the masses. With just two leagues to go, Technicus drew alongside Edsel!

On the final league, Edsel met his downfall. For as he sped neck and neck with Technicus past the imperial reviewing stand, the rim of his right wheel flew apart and a shower of nails and cheap brass sprayed Edsel's face, drawing blood.

Then a carved lion fell from the chariot's front. That hobbled his team; and as they went down, Edsel went over them and into the dirt. Technicus continued unabated, and won clearly.

Caligula, who had been downing huge quantities of wine and fish, fell into spasms and became apoplectic and regurgitated. He clutched his chest and moaned, his face turning the color of spring grapes. Then seeing the turn of events, and hearing the roar of approval for Technicus from the crowd, the temple priest who had been attending Caligula lifted a wooden mallet and dispatched him to the netherworld.

*"That story hit painfully close to home," remarked Satan. "I must ponder it awhile."*

*"May I go, then?" asked the prisoner.*

*"Don't leave just yet. I have a few questions. First, do you know what 'the netherworld' means?"*

*"Hell, Hades, here. This is the netherworld."*

*"And," the devil continued, "do you think Caligula was actually dispatched here?"*

*"I just added that phrase for dramatic effect," claimed the prisoner. "It was merely a plot device."*

*"Oh no, it wasn't. It is true." The devil was becoming somber, almost morose.*

*"Caligula has been here for centuries," Satan confessed. "He has tenure now and is irreplaceable, although there's a rumor circulating that he's got his resume on the street. We do not refer to him by his former name, however. We call him Reflecto."*

*"Your assistant? The man in the silver suit?"*

*"One and the same. A tireless worker, yet he maintains one deli-*

*ciously twisted sense of humor. Ever wonder why he wears that welder's helmet? He's tired of getting knocked on the head with a wooden mallet."*

*Silence followed. The prisoner, still astonished, said nothing. Neither did the devil. Standing outside, listening through the door, Reflecto noticed the prolonged stillness and became worried. He cautiously opened the door and stuck his head inside the chamber, his hand still rubbing the rising welt on his forearm.*

*"Is everything all right, sir? Sir?"*

*"Reflecto."*

*"Yes, sir. At your service."*

*"Reflecto, your suit is looking a little ratty, man. But you're in luck. You see, I'm suddenly in a generous mood. Take a few dollars from petty cash and buy a new one. And I mean spend it all on a nice suit! Stay away from the wine and fish, you hear?"*

*Reflecto cursed under his breath and grabbed the fourth prisoner's arm. "Come on," he mumbled. "Let's get the hell out of here."*

# THE LOST CULT OF CONSENSUS
## (TEAMWORK *IN* EXTREMIS)

" . . . it must make any set of people, whether freemen
or slaves, split into factions, at feud with one another and
incapable of any joint action?"

**Plato**, *Republic*

*As soon as the fifth prisoner entered the devil's throne room, a terse
command emanated from the darkness. "Sit down. Over there, on the
bench!"*

*He looked about and found it, the only piece of furniture in the dusky
chamber. It was spare, utilitarian, without frills, and offering no comfort.
Very inoffensive design, thought the prisoner, very acceptable. He sat
and waited.*

*"I have been reading," said the devil, "reading of lost civilizations
and ancient mysteries. I have been wondering, too."*

*Prisoner number five squirmed on the polished wooden seat, won-
dering himself. What was the beast getting to?*

*"I have wondered why some civilizations flower on earth, then per-
ish, without leaving so much as a trace. What happened to the
Anasazi—the native Americans from the deserts of Arizona? Or the
Mexican Olmecs, the ones who built great pyramids centuries before
the Aztecs or the Mayans?"*

*Prisoner number five was a human resource executive, specifically
responsible for team-building and focus groups and consensus-building in a huge corporation. And he had no idea what the evil one was*

*speaking of. He decided to listen further.*

*"Aside from a few potsherds and some carved stone, we know nothing of these peoples."*

*"I know nothing of them either, dark prince. I study modern civilizations: teams, work groups, focus units, corporate culture."*

*"Do you like the bench you sit upon?"*

*The prisoner shook his head in confusion. The devil was moving too fast, jumping from subject to subject. It would be difficult to keep up. Finally, he nodded, yes. The bench was suitable.*

*"It is a Shaker bench, lowly expert on human resources. It is all function and no form. All use—no art. No embellishments; no personal, individual touches whatsoever."*

*"Very nice," muttered the HR exec, rubbing his hand over the simple planks. "But I was told you wanted to hear about team-building, reaching consensus in modern business settings. What has the bench or the ancient, mysterious Aztecs to do with that?"*

*Satan hissed in disdain. Here, the depraved genius thought, is living proof of management malfeasance. Here is a specialist in corporate culture with no knowledge of other cultures. Then he snarled his response. "The Shakers, fool! They are lost as well. Do you not know of the Shakers?"*

*"No sir, I must confess, I have no knowledge or opinion on them."*

*The devil choked back his exasperation and launched into a condescending lecture, not unlike a bored professor.*

*"The Shakers were a religious cult, idiot. They originated in England in 1747, but made a grand colony a century later in Kentucky. Shakers were a millenarian sect, practicing celibacy and an ascetic community life. It doesn't take a human resource executive to determine why they died out."*

*"Why was that?" asked the prisoner.*

*"Start with the word* celibacy, *sludge brain. Separating men and*

*women is great for social control, but it tends to reduce future genera-*
*tions. But, as you can see, those Shakers made tremendous hand-*
*wrought furniture! Examples fill your museums and finer homes to this*
*day. Now we know why a group of a few hundred souls produced over*
*one hundred thousand chairs," added Satan. "There was no sex. They*
*took it out on the wood!"*

*"My story is similar, sir," cried out the prisoner, elated to see a*
*sort of devil-executive consensus building so quickly. "I tell of another*
*little-known sect, the Consensii, with an equally unnatural belief.*
*They left no great pyramids, no astonishing astronomy. But they were*
*unique. For although the Incas and Aztecs, the Mayans, and the other*
*ancient Mesoamerican peoples never applied the wheel to commerce*
*or industry, the Consensii invented the round table."*

*He waited, hoping the devil would signal his pleasure, or at least*
*his agreement.*

*"The round table, eh?" asked the devil. "Perhaps that did for*
*them what celibacy did for the Shakers."*

*"What's that?"*

*"Nice furniture, but no future. Ha, Ha, Ha!"*

*"I think you're right, sir. I think we may have some interesting*
*team dynamics going, right here, right in this conversation."*

*"Shut up with your pseudo-speak and start telling the story!"*

*Prisoner number five nervously cleared his throat and began to*
*recite from his notes.*

e begin this quest for the lost cult of Consensus with
their remains. Digs have recovered their art, if it can
be called such. For it is so mundane and bland. No col-
ors, no impressions, and nothing that might be considered the slightest bit offensive. The Consensii made art that would

appeal to everyone. This explains its consistent drabness.

Their dwellings appear of uniform height and constant size, it being offensive for one family to have a habitat more commodious than others. Figurines are very unusual, however. Every one of them is smiling. Animals, gods, half-beast-half-man statues, they are often ferocious, but they all smile pleasantly. In Consensus, it seems, being angry or disagreeable was sinful.

As for their diet, the same pattern emerges. How to describe it? Phlegmatic? Maybe it's best to suggest it would have made English cooking seem spicy, stimulating. They ate communally, you see, and so as not to offend the tastes of a single member, they dined on gruel and raw corn, always.

Evidence confirms their belief in the lowest common denominator, no matter how empty and dull. One can only imagine their music and rituals. Some suggest a Consensii orgy and a Consensii wake to have been the same. And a Consensii orchestra to have consisted of one drummer beating a stick against a rock, staccato, and quietly. How did this banality get started, anyway?

Their founder, a man called Innocuous, broke off from the Aztecs around 1500 A.D. This is understandable, for the Aztecs were wild, vengeful, and disturbingly moody. They covered their cities, particularly Mexico, with the blood of human sacrifices. And they wore colorful mantles of parrot feathers and jaguar skins. They used gaudy, obsidian-tipped blades to decapitate war prisoners and built mountains of skulls to appease their gods. Revolted, Innocuous bolted.

He fled to the jungles and took one thousand former prisoners and slaves, along with some disaffected Aztec chiefs. They would build a new society, one where no one was better nor worse than the other. Where the ostentatious were shunned, and to stand out was to stand apart. Where everyone shared equally and everyone agreed on everything, or it would not be done. They would call it the community of *Consensus.*

Consensii leaders would be elected by unanimous vote, and thus must appease the wants and whims of every single citizen. All new ideas or projects would be brought to the round table and there discussed. Every citizen, of all persuasions and abilities, would then opine as to his or her view. Arguments in favor and in opposition would be scrawled on nearby rocks for all to see and comment upon.

The flower growers, for example, would suggest more fields given to their plants than to the corn planters. The round table would be rolled out, and the entire community would drop tools and weapons and scurry to the meeting place. Days would pass. Ballots would be taken and retaken. And flowers would wilt and corn parch.

Or Innocuous would be petitioned to name a certain day the feast of a minor god or another. Then came the round table, the dropping of work, and the endless consensus-building. At the end of a month, it would be agreed that every single citizen could name a god for the honor. This explains why, even though there were then, as now, 365 days in a year, the Consensii had 1174 feast days.

And, of course, no god could be greater or lesser than the others, nor its stela higher or lower, nor its color brighter or flatter. The lowest common denominator reigned in Consensus—in all things, for all people, alike.

How then to explain the disappearance of such a gentle, agreeable cult? Four popular books have appeared recently to do just that. Their conclusions are all believable, yet each different.

*Theory One: The Hungry Jaguar.*
A sentry stationed on the edge of the Consensii encampment was sprung upon by a ravenous jaguar. Before those nearby could agree on how to save their comrade, the animal had bitten away his right arm and disappeared with it into the foliage.

At the next scheduled meeting of the round table, it was agreed that being one-armed was a distinct disadvantage for the sentry. So in order to achieve equality, and because a new arm could not be attached, all citizens agreed to tie their right arm behind their back (amputation being too reminiscent of the Aztecs).

This accomplished, the one-armed Consensii went on with their affairs, though a bit less efficiently, until a quarryman was pinned between two stones being cut for the image of yet another god. Regrettably, his left arm was severed. Out came the round table— and the ropes. How long did it take for the armless Consensii to starve? Three days, maximum.

*Theory Two: Montezuma's Revenge.*

Angered at the desertion of the Consensii, the Aztec leader Montezuma sent a raiding party through the steaming jungles and into their village. Alarmed, the inhabitants called for a hasty meeting and gathered around the table to discuss defensive strategy. Finding them so grouped, in the open and occupied with discussion, the Aztecs went through them like an obsidian scythe through standing wheat.

*Theory Three: Didn't We Forget About Something?*

A particularly difficult issue flared, something such as how many parrots each family might keep as pets, and a round table discussion was called. Because they're involved, the parrots were invited and joined in the discussion. But like their owners, the parrots were repetitive and unyielding in their comments. The linguistic equivalent of an endless computer loop ensued.

Months passed in circular debate, and the corn crop, standing unattended, rotted in the fields. In desperation, the hungry Consensii took another week to decide to eat the parrots. But the parrots dissented vehemently, so the motion was tabled and the people starved. And the parrots flew away.

*Theory Four: A Whole Lot of Shaking Going On.*

This theory is somewhat bawdy, but given the Shakers in Kentucky, not too far-fetched. It seems the question of sexual prowess and practices was placed on a round table agenda. Consensii offered their opinions on how and how often copulation should occur between husband and wife. Witnesses were called, testimony was eagerly taken.

Wide discrepancies surfaced regarding individual practices, methodology, and results. How should the union of man and woman take place? they pondered; and, as we can imagine, this led to tremendously long and detailed argument and elaboration.

A pre-Columbian gridlock resulted. To break the debate and get back to the corn fields lest they starve, Innocuous, in his one act of decisiveness, proclaimed the topic "tabled". Sex would not take place until the matter was resolved to everyone's satisfaction. And the Consensii went down the same disappointing path the Shakers would take centuries later—to become the frustrated and the forgotten.

"*Are those the only theories?*" *asked Satan.*

"*Yes, malicious master. And of the four, the last has sold the most books.*"

"*No doubt. But what of the message left by the lost cult of Consensus? It is universal, swine. And timely. Even you, a mere mortal, should know this. The lure of consensus is not restricted to* the Yucatan Peninsula or to the time of this tale. It abounds in modern businesses at this very time. All you've done is amuse me, which is more than most HR slugs could ever do. But you haven't distilled a lesson from the tale."

"Beware of consensus?" offered the timid executive.

"Bingo!" the devil exclaimed. "Consensus can be the divine frost of the competitive jungle—it may be cool, but it will freeze your group into inaction. Remember this: when the balm of agreement is overused, it becomes the coagulant of progress. Things stop. The oil of compromise can lead to the rusting of individual responsibility."

"Then much of what I've been doing—all this team-building and consensus-making and focus-grouping—was it a foolish pursuit?" asked the HR executive.

"Not entirely," answered the devil. "It is furniture making—beneficial up to a certain point. After that, as the Shakers would tell us, it gets in the way of real action. It's like celibacy, too."

"How's that?"

"It's best when it comes to an end."

While the devil laughed and stamped his feet in glee at this final piece of wisdom, prisoner number five was led away.

Alone, Satan pondered the drabness of his surroundings, the sameness of pain and anguish, never changing, never ending. And so it would be, he realized, forever. The Demon Decorating Committee, meeting weekly for decades, handled the interior design. The Steering Group on Sin had to approve all deviant behavior, and the evil that was once outlandishly novel was now merely dull. And the Task Force for Moral Turpitude was still debating the vices they'd been discussing for centuries. They still thought sloth and usury were exciting! No wonder they call this place Hell, he concluded. Then he drew himself up on his throne, abandoned these depressive notions, and decided to act.

68

*"Reflecto!" he roared. "Cancel every committee meeting on the schedule! Disband every task force and steering group. Dissolve the focus teams, and eliminate the leadership round table!"*

*Reflecto beamed with joy and couldn't help responding. "Wonderful, sir, just wonderful! I think we've got a terrific line-staff management dynamic going here!"*

*"Shut up, bullet-head! I'll handle the mockery here," Satan sputtered through a smile. "Whenever I hear that soft and fuzzy rot, I can't decide whether to laugh or throw up!"*

*"Sometimes when you do one, it sounds like the other," Reflecto whispered under his breath.*

*"I heard that!" the devil shot back. "Now, get out of here, will ya? Go get me another human resource!"*

# THE LABYRINTH OF BULL
## (WHERE BUREAUCRACY IS KING)

"In the great crises of life, and in the great problems of conduct and belief, we trust to our feelings rather than to our diagrams."
—**Jean Jacques Rousseau**, *Confessions*

*As soon as the sixth prisoner laid down his pencil, an evil underling snatched him by his collar and pulled him from his chair. While the silver-suited assistant fumbled with a key in the prisoner's ankle manacle, another tied a blindfold over his eyes. Prisoner number six was pushed and pulled, stumbling as he went, from the writing cell and forced down a seemingly unending series of winding corridors and maze-like passageways.*

*He became dizzy with all the turns and changes of direction. Shoves and grunts were the only guides, rude slaps and kicks the only response to his questions. "Where are we?" he kept asking. "Where am I going?" They would not answer, except with another shove.*

*After hours of bewilderment and bruises, prisoner number six heard a eerie creaking, followed by a metallic clang. Unbeknownst to him, he had just entered the devil's throne room. The sound of retreating footsteps told him he was being left alone there, and the ominous thud of thrown bolts confirmed it. He stood there, sightless, confused, terrified.*

*"Welcome to my world," came a sinister voice, rasping of breath, threatening.*

*"Where am I?" squealed the prisoner.*

*"You should feel at home," he heard. Then came a low moaning from somewhere in the darkness, making his skin crawl. "Walk forward!"*

*Prisoner number six took three blind, tentative steps to his front and was then knocked backwards to the floor. A door had been slammed in his face.*

*"Get to your feet!" commanded the voice. "Turn left, take four paces."*

*The frightened executive did as he was told, counting each step. The fourth step, though, ended in empty air. His foot sank and his body followed. He had fallen into a fetid pit. Slithering things groped at him, and he flailed his arms in the dark, desperately trying to orient himself and claw his way out of the hole.*

*When he found his way to a slippery wall and pulled himself out, the voice ordered him to come toward it. Hesitating, flinching at each step, the man complied. "Stick out your right hand," he was told. "There is a gift for you."*

*The prisoner slowly raised his arm and reached into the unseen, fingers feeling the torrid air, clenching and unclenching as his hand groped forward into the unknown void. He felt something hard, cold; then heard a slight click, a sudden snap. Bolts of pain shot up his arm, and he jerked back his hand in anguish. Prisoner number six had put his hand into a steel-jawed rat trap.*

*He pranced about convulsively, shaking and pulling the trap from his hand. Finally it was gone, flung away into the never-ending darkness, clattering across the stone.*

*"Why are you doing this to me?" he begged the unseen torturer. "What have I done to deserve this?"*

*The devil answered immediately. "Let's see if this registers in your dull mind:* Not Invented Here.*"*

*The prisoner said nothing.*

"Hello," continued Satan, rapping his knuckles on his throne. "Anybody home?"

Prisoner number six, though still blinded, suddenly began to see the light. For on earth, the man had built a bureaucracy of the first order. A pyramid of power so baffling and impenetrable that, though it provided him comfort and satisfaction, it was virtually frozen in inactivity. And he himself was a master of the Not-Invented-Here syndrome.

When he had found himself cramped in the devil's organization, when he found himself chained inside a cubicle little bigger than a box on one of his intricate charts, prisoner number six began to worry. Then he had found his writing assignment. Across the first page of his pad was written one word: "Bull".

The devil told him to remove his blindfold so he could read the resulting story. But first, Satan advised him, he would have to answer a question or two.

"You were a champion of structure," the voice began. "You were a master of complexity and intricacy. Structure! Structure! Structure! That was your idol, wasn't it, dullard?"

"But sir, structure is paramount in modern organizations. Structure supports efficiency."

"When does structure cease to support and start to strangle?" the devil shot back. "When do organizations become so intricate they ossify and break at the touch of change?"

Prisoner number six considered his answer very carefully, as always, then decided to cover his ass, as always.

"You, oh perverse one, you must tell me. I am simply here to learn from you."

"Bull!" shouted the devil, instantly enraged. "You are here to give me wisdom, stooge! Now take off that damned blindfold and tell me of bureaucracy, and of bull, and of how complexity in any *organization is simply a way of building hell on earth!"*

*Prisoner number six, pleased that the interrogation was over, strained to focus his eyes in the dim light of hellfire. As he read the words came into sharp focus. The message, born of confusion, assumed a crystal clarity.*

he bull has always been a symbol of ponderous weight and clumsy thinking, and I have chosen to use this metaphor in two ways. For the bull is not only the unthinking animal, brutish and without skill, but it is the institution that houses it. I shall tell of both. I shall begin in the ancient world.

In Greek mythology, the island of Crete was the home of the bull and of the king who thought like one.

Recent digs have revealed thousands of tablets describing rigid hierarchy and systematic administration near Knossos, on Crete. And archaeologists have found great statues of bulls there, everywhere. The center of this real civilization was a labyrinth, a puzzle palace of passageways designed to baffle mortals. Bureaucracy and bull are joined here, as are fact and myth. And the resultant structure is appalling.

The Minoans had Crete, they had Cyprus, and thousands of islands in the Mediterranean and Aegean Seas. And they had a good and kind King: Minos I. He planned carefully and provided for the education and well-being of all citizens, and they loved him for it. He encouraged trade and supported the arts. In all things Minos I was wise. But Minos I made one mistake. Minos I begat Minos II. The bull was born.

Minos II was a different kind of king. He was possessive as a child, and frightened. He assumed the wealth of his peoples to be fixed and his task to protect it from without. He became defensive. He built the ultimate defense mechanism: the Labyrinth.

What a palace it was! Huge, sprawling, filled with passages and doorways and small rooms without number. The architects and builders were made to construct baffles and corridors leading to nowhere, and a bewildering array of entrances and vestibules. Seen from the sky, the Labyrinth was a maze without compare. Legend has it that once in, no mortal could escape. Minos II dwelt securely within.

It was the center of government, too. And so into the chambers without number went administrators without number. They were segregated through complex and arcane rules, allowing those who did a particular thing to locate in a particular place, and none other.

These places were given ominous names: divisions, departments, bureaus, offices, commissions, branches. And the minions working within each were called secretaries and deputies, assistants, clerks, attachés, liaisons, and sometimes various combinations, like under-assistant-deputy and co-executive-liaison-clerk.

This is just the beginning. For the people so classified per-formed exotic rituals. They interfaced, they coordinated, they reviewed and approved. They were known to touch base and get involved, and even to ride in huge steering committees. But they derived the greatest delight from other activities. They tabled, and postponed, and they wove elaborate hidden agendas. The Minoans were most imaginative.

All this was being directed by Minos II, who sat in a great throne room in the center of the Labyrinth. Minos II had a special bull, too. It lurked around corners, defending the status quo. It was Minos II's secret. Should anyone penetrate the bewildering vanguards, the bull would charge him.

Though he did nothing himself, Minos II kept commanding more walls, more administrators, more under-assistant-deputies. So over the years, the labyrinth became so intricate that Minos II and all of his minions could not have left had they the inclination. The way out had long since been lost. The puzzle palace was complete. They felt safe inside, for that is where their world was. The outside, as far as they were concerned, didn't exist.

But it did, beyond the walls and past the hive. And from the outside three wise ones approached one evening, seeking to trade with the Minoans and impart knowledge of the rest of the earth.

When word reached Minos II, he erupted in anger. "Who are they?" he screamed at his assistant-co-executive message bearer.

"One is named Whodini, and he is acclaimed as an artist of evasion. He has wit and skill and has escaped from Athens where he was held in bondage. Whodini vows to free you, dear king, from your entrapment. And he pledges to bring the world of knowledge through these mazes and into your mind."

"Bull!" shouted Minos II. "It can't be done. And besides, we have enough evasiveness here! But who are the others?"

"The second is a navigator late of the North seas. He calls himself Magneto, and carries a strange device."

"A weapon? A treasure? What is this apparatus he bears?"

"He styles it a bull detector, my lord. He claims it indicates the direction from which bull emanates, and he uses it to flee charging bulls."

"Bull!" screamed Minos II. And he was indignant, for no one knew from which passageway or down which corridor the bull in the labyrinth would charge.

"The third wise one, sir, is a woman."

"So? What brings her to bother us?"

"She is called the puzzle master, your bullness, and she professes a talent for deciphering procedures and simplifying what has been made enigmatic."

"This is the greatest threat our land has ever faced!" Minos II shouted to all present. "We cannot allow foreign thoughts, fresh ideas, or new approaches! None of these tools or talents have been invented here!" Then he spat out a profanity: They are NIH!" The courtiers present gasped. NIH, they knew, was *Not Invented Here*, a curse so vile it surpassed blasphemy! NIH was evil. NIH was lower than bull droppings.

Minos bellowed a command: "We must not allow such fiends to upset the labyrinth!" Then he nodded down to his deputy-co-chair-assistant and whispered, "Give them the treatment, in kind with their threat." The minion smiled and, rubbing his hands together in glee, left.

Outside the perimeter the three wise ones waited with pleasant expectations. They had heard of the Labyrinth and knew their services would be needed within. Then suddenly they were enveloped in a web of paper and red tape thrown down from a parapet. Tied and straining to break free, they were placed in separate chambers to await their fates.

The navigator's trial began almost at once. Three hundred and sixty acting-deputy-co-executive administrators were assembled in a great circle within an immense conference room. Once arranged at every point of the compass, a minion at each degree, the navigator was placed within the center.

"There is bull in here!" announced a deputy-communications-liaison. All 360 minions smiled. Then the speaker tossed the acclaimed bull detector into the center of the ring, where it was caught by Magneto. "Find the bull in two minutes!" the speaker barked. "Or meet your death!

Magneto confidently removed the bull detector's protective cover and looked at its dial. But rather than wiggling a bit, like a compass needle, and settling in a definite alignment, the detector's directional arrow began to circle, and to pick up speed. Around and around it went, the baffled navigator having trouble following it with his eyes. Soon it was spinning faster than an airplane propeller, pointing first to one labyrinthian and then another, then another, then seemingly in all directions at once.

The minions stood in their taunting ring and laughed. The navigator whirled in their center and suddenly fell dead, an arrow through his neck. No one knew from which direction it came. But since his time was up, they all claimed credit for the shot. All 360 rushed to their cubicles to author self-serving memos-to-the-file elucidating their singular bravery and hinting at the possibility of a merit increase in salary.

The next day the escape artist was brought into a large sunlit courtyard, his hands unbound and his clothing removed. These same 360 minions ringed the area, sitting in folding chairs, each holding a fist-sized rock. "They claim you can escape any pursuer," called a voice from the crowd. The sun was beating down fiercely, it being just after noon, and Whodini had to squint to see the speaker. "You have the remainder of the day to elude the chaser at your feet," someone shouted, "or die trying."

Whodini looked about and saw no one. Aside from the minions on the perimeter, the clearing was absolutely empty, save for him. Where was this mystery pursuer? Then he glanced down at the pavement under his feet and saw it. His shadow.

And of course, as he moved so did his shadow with him. He pranced and flipped, turned somersaults, stood on his hands, everything he could possibly imagine, but there being not a cloud in the sky, the shadow stayed with him.

All the while the minions roared in amusement. And, as nature would have it, Whodini's dark pursuer lengthened as the afternoon wore one. Finally, in desperation and defeat, Whodini pleaded to the crowd. "I give up," he screamed. "I will never escape my own shadow!"

Just then, as though by prearranged agreement, 360 rocks came hurtling from the perimeter upon the frustrated captive. Their cumulative effect, of course, was fatal. And only when he fell to the earth *in extremis,* his corpse covered by thrown stones, did his shadow actually disappear.

No one had given the order to kill the outsider, but as the senior-lieutenant-lapidary lofter announced, there were no rules broken here. No one of the 360 had killed the man. No one is killed by a single stone, he explained to them all. No one acted out of order. No one was responsible. All sighed in relief at this conclusion. Whodini may not have eluded his shadow, but each of them had masterfully escaped their responsibility. All rejoiced.

The puzzle master was next.

"We pray you are the woman wizard," began the deputy-spokesperson-for-bondage-studies. "We have a challenge you shall respect!" Then they all roared in glee and bellicosity, and in came a wheeled cart laden with tablets.

Thousands of tablets, all inscribed with fine detail. All linked and cross-referenced and indexed, and some in three parts, and others referring to tablets in other rooms and other lands. "This is our triumph," boasted the clerk-of-make-work. "This is our procedure for breathing! We shall give you thirty days to understand it and follow it, then we shall check on your conformance."

But then he paused, took a breath of the foul air himself, and added a final condition. "But since you are a puzzle decoder, we will gag you and fill your nostrils with wax. Then you will have incentive to follow the procedure correctly! But you have thirty days, so take your time!" Wild snorting and chortling followed this last remark, and the woman was so bound and gagged.

And, of course, she perished. For researchers had spent lifetimes writing the procedure, and it was airtight. No one could understand it, and so they thought it a success.

The torture thus quietly ended, all work and play resumed throughout the Labyrinth. No visitors appeared, and no inhabitants left. The walls were too strong, the processes too Byzantine.

And then the bull went crazy.

No one knows what precipitated this calamity. Some suggest he sniffed a cow passing the Labyrinth. Some that he grew tired of Minos II. Others that the bull finally realized there was more to life than wandering down blind alleys and catching bureaucrats making personal phone calls or reading romance novels. In any case, he went on a rampage.

Thousands of minions were thus upset and pinioned against walls or stamped into the floor or gored. Dozens would huddle in a hopefully forgotten room praying the bull would pass them over. Yet he found every single one. Through random chargings and his animal instincts, the entire population of imprisoned Minoans was extinguished. All but Minos II. He was alive at the end, lurking in hallways and stumbling into department after department with no clue as to his whereabouts. Then he was spotted.

The giant bull lowered his head and began to charge toward Minos II, bellowing as he came down a corridor. Minos II ducked through a doorway and down another passage, but the bull came on, closer now. The king and the bull thus ran through the maze from one end to the next, the bull snorting and panting and the King screaming as he stumbled over the corpses.

"Help me" he pleaded. "Help me out of here!" But, of course, no one could escape the king's maze. He had made certain of this himself.

"Give me the navigator!" he begged as he ran, the bull hiding in wait, somewhere, "Give me the bull detector, and I can evade this ravenous beast!" But, of course, the bull detector was NIH, and had spun itself into pieces long ago.

"Puzzle master! Puzzle master! I beg you decipher the maze— we shall both be free." But, of course, she was also NIH, and had not drawn a breath for years.

"Where is Whodini, my favorite escape artist? Where is that genius, that wonderful man whom I shall make king as we pass through the last door?" But, of course, Whodini had also been NIH and was too stoned to answer the call.

So in desperation, the king pivoted and confronted the slobbering bull head-on. And he firmly grasped the horns of the beast with both hands and held them tightly. "I have the bull by the horns," he howled proudly. "I have the bull by the horns at last!" But the bull didn't buy it. "I've got the king by the hands," screamed the bull.

The bull reared his head and shook Minos II and slammed him against a wall. And he kept thrusting his head and waving his horns and smashing him into every division and partition in the maze, thudding the still clinging Minos II to pieces.

Then basking in self-pride, his horns still draped with the bloody dross that was left of Minos II, the great bull began to speak.

"I am immortal" he cried out, his new voice echoing down the endless halls. "I shall leave this place and find my kind and multiply and cover the earth. And we shall reign supreme for all time!"

*"A wonderful tale," pronounced the devil, "full of stupidity and pride, fear and crime. I like those kind of stories."*

*"I am honored you find it appealing."*

"But, one question," Satan responded. "Is the story really of ancient origin, or is it a modern fable?"

"It's part history, part myth, sir. As old as stone."

"And here you are wrong, insect," snarled Satan. "The bull is everywhere, alive and multiplying to this day! The bull who wrecked the Labyrinth was correct: he never dies. Giant corporations have erected labyrinths of confusion and puzzles of procedures. So have governments and institutions of all types. And minions still dwell in defined little segments, with defined little viewpoints. They continue to claim credit for tasks they've not done and evade responsibility for the things they have.

"In these labyrinths," Satan continued, "anything from the outside is treated as inferior—it's NIH—be it client, customer, competitor. By the same logic, anything from within these labyrinths is thought superior, be it dumb, dangerous or destructive. And the walls keep going up around these places. And the bull roams within them, supreme."

"Reflecto!" he yelled once the prisoner had exited. "Send in the next captive. But make it someone different. These whining idiots are getting on my nerves. Bring me someone fresh and unexpected—someone particularly repulsive—someone really NIH!"

"As you wish," the silver-suited sycophant answered. "I have just such an offender in mind."

CHAPTER 7

# THE TELL-TALE TELEX
## (SHAME IS A MANAGEMENT SKILL)

"I heard many things in hell. How, then, am I mad?
Hearken! and observe how healthily—
how calmly I can tell you the whole story."

**—Edgar Allen Poe**, *The Tell-Tale Heart*

*From his perch in the corner of the writing room, just inside the door, Reflecto monitored the labors of the remaining penitents. Delicate scratchings, pausing and then returning, echoed from cubicle to cubicle. The executives were writing, some with labored strokes, others pouring out stories with the abandon of the condemned.*

*From a corner spot, however, came nothing but silence, then sobbing. Reflecto angled his laser-like vision off a ceiling mirror and spied the man within.*

*Elbows on the desk, head in hands, this captive was enveloped in anguish. Reflecto zoomed his attention to the pad. It was rippled with moisture, spotted with dripping perspiration. Then the assignment for the story came into view. A single word:* Shame. *The man was not perspiring at all. He was weeping. Reflecto rose from his station and approached him.*

*"I felt you coming," the prisoner told Reflecto as he entered the cubicle. "I felt your eye, your evil eye, peering down on me with disgust."*

*"And you have written nothing, cretin!" Reflecto shouted. "Time is wasting, man! At this rate we'll never get out of here!"*

*"We* will *never get out of here?" the prisoner inquired.*

*"I mean* you *will never escape, neither you nor your associates!"*

*corrected Reflecto, shocked that he'd let his true intentions slip so foolishly. "What is the problem?"*

*"I just can't write about it," complained the prisoner.*

*"About what?" asked Reflecto.*

*"About me. About my shameful acts. I know what I've done, and I know it's wrong. But I'm a businessman—not a writer. I need help," he begged. "I need help badly."*

*Reflecto snorted in disgust and backed out of the cubicle. In moments he was back, slamming a leather-bound volume on the desk, next to the sodden writing tablet.*

*"Use this as a guide," he ordered. "It's his favorite author."*

*The prisoner lifted the heavy book and carefully examined its title:* The Collected Works of Edgar Allen Poe. *Then he opened it and noticed a sales receipt used as a page marker. Strange. Aspen, Colorado, was printed on the slip. He scanned the contents, whispering the titles.*

"The Pit and the Pendulum. Premature Burial. The Murders in the Rue Morgue—*No wonder he likes Poe," he said. "This stuff sounds right up his alley."*

*"Indeed it is," replied Reflecto. "Read the introduction," he then commanded, "and you will understand why." The prisoner opened the book and began to read aloud.*

*"'In October of 1849 a semiconscious man was found in a side street outside a polling place in Baltimore. He was incoherent, ragged. Reeking of liquor, he was rushed to a hospital. But alas, after several days he failed to regain consciousness, and expired. He was one of the greatest writers and thinkers American literature has to offer. He was Edgar Allen Poe, dead at age 40.*

*Poe is the father of the psychological horror tale, and a brilliant, though deeply troubled romanticist. What educated citizen has not read his* Tell-Tale Heart, The Raven, *or* The Murders in the Rue

Morgue? *Who has not ached with longing and shuddered in melancholy at the sound of his haunting "Annabel Lee"?*

*And why is Poe so frightening, even to us, today? He presents few monsters, no mutants, and no ravenous beasts. He deals chiefly with humans, their guilt, and their shame. This explains the power of his horror. And its universality.*

*For Poe exposed shame. He pulled it from the hidden recesses of the psyche and described it in black and white. His genius is that every reader, of every time, recognizes it as his or her own. It is the monster we sleep with, and Poe gave it size and shape—and a voice.*

*Shame has been described as a selective force in human evolution. It keeps us from aberrant and species-threatening actions. It keeps us from reverting to the jungle, lusting in greedy heat for anything and everything. Sometimes.'"*

"*But shame has no place in business,*" the prisoner offered, setting down the tome and looking up into the gaze of his silver-clad guard. "*Shame is a handicap, an irrelevancy. The dollar is the thing, and what has Poe, a droll depressive from Victorian times, to know of today's commerce and technology?*"

"*Now you know why stories are important,*" Reflecto answered. "*From stories come wisdom that can never be projected onto the screen of a conference room.*"

The prisoner shook his head in puzzlement, but Reflecto continued, his patience wearing thin. "*Read* The Tell-Tale Heart," he ordered. "*Then write of shame.*"

By the time the prisoner finished scrawling his very personal tale, Reflecto was standing at his shoulder again, eager to escort him to the devil's inquisition chamber. And once there, Satan himself was just as eager to get on with the storytelling.

"*My assistant tells me I should enjoy this one,*" he hissed from the dark recesses of his lair. "*So pray it confronts evil and heinous crimes. And," he added, "Pray it confronts them in your soul."*

*The prisoner stifled his fear, assumed the voice of a narrator, and began.*

P lease allow me to introduce myself. I'm a man of wealth and haste. I've laid many a company bare to pile up profit and purge out waste. You may think me intelligent, but I am not; I'm crafty, street-smart. I don't read books, I wring assets for every drop of worth I can. The last books I've read were Classic Comics, kid's versions of the old, irrelevant gasps of paupers.

I buy and streamline companies. I cut out the fat, I optimize the rest. In the rat race, my friends, I am the fastest rat. And the leanest one.

They saw that in Baltimore, when I turned an ailing hospital around by squeezing the charity cases so hard the ink turned from red to black in six months. Red is the color of bleeding hearts. Black is the color of mine, and I bring it to the bottom line. And that's all that matters. They cheer me for it.

From that poor beginning, I made my name. And I made my mark on companies sitting on fat assets and undervalued products. I am, my friends, not crazy. I am crafty.

And the list keeps growing. First it was petrochemicals, a mature industry with no room for growth. Ha! I spied hidden treasure everywhere! I moved processing plants offshore, to friendly, business-tolerant lands. I put our chemical operations in Burma, land of ten-cent labor and a winking government. Minimized assets plus zero maintenance equals maximized profit. The formula of the crafty.

Or take agribusiness. Waste, storage, high inventory—the marks of ignorance. Product flow is cash flow, it's that simple. I have three theories on asset velocity, my friends: Move it! Move it! Move it! And we did.

When federal regulations blocked the sale of our tainted infant formula in the States, we moved it anyway—to the Third World. They don't care down there. Starving babies aren't finicky. Warehouses cleared out in an instant. I am a magician—I make crap disappear and money levitate—to me!

Modern agribusiness, give me a break! Who cares if it works for low-end grains on the great plains? I feed at the top of the food chain. Give me high-value-added stuff, citrus, bananas, mangoes. Give me barefoot peasants in Latin America who know who's boss. Then turn the patchwork fields of native crops to seas of similarity. Waves of trees, all of a kind, waving value back to me. Volume is king, and the Europeans will jump like monkeys over the fruit I ship—at the cost of peanuts. Let me tell you about craftiness!

Those are but three legs to the stool on which I stand. Together they spell POE, Pan Oceanic Enterprises. This is my kingdom, though I don't know squat about methyloxidane, the La Leche League, or banana republics. I know asset velocity, cash flow, and market turnover. I am a gymnast in global competition, and those are my tricks.

My reach is total, my commands instantaneous. And my ear is always to the ground, searching for trends, weakness, the time to pounce. But staying tethered to the stock ticker, or the fax, or even the cellular phone is demanding, even for me. I run away from time to time. Sometimes it's with a woman, sometimes not. When it's not, it's for a better reason. I need to escape *the eye.*

The eye—the media, the fools on the other end of the wires and airwaves. The stooges who help make me, and the same ones I use to keep my game going. When I want to squeeze a union or get a government exception, I cry foul. Think of the jobs lost. Think of the mom 'n pops without customers. The stories reach their mark. The plant beats the wage increase, the license is approved. The return on assets rises.

And the media, the stupid eye, thinks it's exposing the truth. What fools! They are no more than dumb tools of the trade. I lead them around like barking seals. I am a genius of dissembling and disinformation. I use the eye, though I hate it.

And when the eye gets out of hand, I run and hide. Like I've done tonight. Way beyond the reach of telephones and faxes and couriers and reporters. I head for this place, Heart Lake, in upstate New York. Past the conference center of Sagamore in Lake George, past the main roads, to this cabin.

So here I am, alone. Out of touch with everyone because the heat is on. If they can't reach me, they have no story. If they have no story, I'm safe. Plunder can wait.

No one but Lenore knows I'm here, and she knows how to keep her mouth shut. She knows I can move her from executive assistant to lunch room waitress in a flash. Have her butt slinging hash for tips. Have her kids hustling papers on the street, I can. She knows a good thing when she sees it.

I arrived here in late afternoon, driving up from the city. I lit a fire and threw down the sash, seeking solitude. And the bar is stocked to my specifications. I also specified no electronics—no phones, faxes, not even lights. The electricity is off everywhere. If they want me, they'll have to get through by carrier pigeon. Ha!

But what is that? Are there mice in this place? Raccoons? It's silent now, only the hissing of the logs in the fireplace. But there it is again. I know I heard something. I'd better check out the basement.

God, it's dark down here. But hold on, there's a thin ray of light through a high window. Must be from the boat dock, a lamppost out there. The light shines into the farthest corner, and I follow it. Oh my God! I haven't seen one of those things in years!

It's a Telex machine, a great, clumsy clanking communications terminal. Whoever ran the company that leases this joint must've installed it ages ago, in a seventies attempt to stay in touch. Ha! Those clattering, rattling old printers sounded like pneumatic drills back then, spewing out reams of paper, one thudding letter at a time, from some dope on the other end of the line. Looks like a relic from a wire service. Where's my drink?

That's better, the fire is getting warmer. Imagine those dolts out there running around looking for me, back in the city. You'd think they'd be used to this routine by now. I mean, is this the first time a tanker split a seam and some poor little birds got greased? Then they'll run shots of dummies on beaches spreading hay around, skinny girls cleaning oil from sea gulls, and yap about double hulls. They love a cliché, don't they. They . . .

Wait a minute? Did I touch that thing? Did I turn it on? No, no, I didn't even get to the bottom of the stairs. But there it goes again, that rapping, that rattling. I'm not sure I'm hearing it or imagining it. Sounds like the noise you get when some college kid sits up in first-class, with a Walkman hooked to his head. You can't hear the music, but you can hear the bass notes, their muffled throbbing, that sssshhh-thunk, sssshhh-thunk two seats away. Drives you nuts!

I'd better check on that telex, just in case. As I open the door, the thin ray of light is still there, but something's different. Is that paper? Was that there before?

It is! My God, it moved! What is this, some kind of joke? Where's my lighter? Oh, here we go, let's see what this is. Looks like a headline, just a sentence or two. "Baltimore: Gas Rupture in Burma. Thousands Flee. Employees Cite Poor Maintenance and Lack of Training."

Coulda been here for years. How long have I been standing here, watching this thing? Five, ten minutes? Hasn't moved a bit. Why, look, it isn't even plugged in. Where are the stairs? I'm outta here!

Standing at the top of the stairs in the dark I could swear I just heard another line printed. That dull rapping, tapping sound. That pinging, ratcheting sound. Am I going nuts? Let's look at that old relic one more time.

Kee-rist! Now I know that wasn't there before! "Baltimore: Blight in Honduras Levels Economy. Single Strain Crops Vulnerable. Famine Nears." I must've overlooked it the first time. Yeah, that's it. This machine is deader 'n a rotary phone.

But sitting here by the fire again, I can't help but wonder. Is that news old? Is that damned machine really connected to an outside line? Maybe they just forgot to unhook it. Maybe it runs on batteries or something. Hey! What the hell? I know I hear it now, I'm positive!

Hurry, hurry to the stairs and down into the darkness. Focus, damned eyes, look! There is more. I wasn't hallucinating, I know this wasn't here last time!

"Baltimore: Price Increases Hit Poor Nations. Infant Formula Beyond Reach for Many. Malnutrition Due to Mothers' Watering Down American Formula."

The damned peasants! Don't they know how to breast feed? Don't they know . . . ? There it goes again, there's no mistaking that rattling. "Edgar Allen, chairman of POE, is unavailable for comment."

God Almighty! Now I know they're after me! The eye, the damned eye will be combing every cabin in these mountains, after my hide! They've probably got Lenore on a rack! Wait! Is that a helicopter outside? Tell me I'm hearing things!

Run, run up the stairs and throw open the sash! Search the sky for lights! There, there it is. They're driving up the road, they're coming after me. What is it, a skylink van? What is this? RAVEN Courier Service? This is the last time I'll tell Lenore where I'm going. Nevermore!

Give him five bucks and get the damned package and shut the door. And be thankful it wasn't CBS or ABC. Can you believe it? I almost jumped outta my skin, and it's just an envelope from Lenore. But then the message: "They are coming soon to interview you, sir. I tried to stop them, but they must have had someone follow your car."

She's dead when I get back to town! Okay, now who will it be? Safer? Jennings? Geraldo? Wait, here comes another car.

I can see the equipment, I can tell it's the eye. I can't run, must be calm, must dissemble. I can disinform, I can control spin, I can and I must! Just a tired exec meditating in the woods. That's all.

But they aren't here to grill me over the Burma leak, the Honduran blight, or even the milk tempest. They want to interview me for an executive lifestyles section. Those unsuspecting fools. Those drivel-peddling nobodies. Ha!

I pace and respond, pace and respond. They jot down notes and take a few flash snaps. It's like throwing sardines to seals. It'll be over in a few minutes. What is that sound? Don't tell me the damned thing in the basement is on again! God, it's getting louder. Surely they hear it.

I move to the kitchen, drawing them away from the door, so casual, so nonchalant. And I speak louder, over the rattling, the chattering, but it gets louder and more rapid, more incessant!

Surely they hear it, the idiots have to hear it! Are they ignoring it, are they mocking me, torturing me? It sounds like a machine gun! How can they keep up the charade? When will they finally admit it? Lifestyles, my ass! They're here to crucify me!

I can't even think. What are they saying? Why are they laughing?

Are they waiting for a whole roll of paper to run itself through, listing all the gruesome details? Are they recording my ticks, my fidgeting, my sweat? Are they reveling in this—pinning me to a wall, watching me squirm?

All right, all right! I surrender! Take the damned stairs and get the Telex! It's all there, every last bit, I'm sure. Take it all down, you damned hungry eye, you!

But they don't move, pretending to be shocked at my outburst.

Here, I shout, come down here and get it over with. Read about the cost of my greed! Write about the payoffs and the deferred maintenance, write of the midnight shipments of formula, of the product dumping at dirt-cheap prices, just to get them weaned off breast feeding and hooked on the crap we make!

Tell all about the plowing under of indigenous crops, about how we forced subsistence farmers to grow huge surpluses—of plants that can't take it down there! Tell it all, boys and girls, tell it to the bloody world! But turn off that blasted telex, this instant! There's enough there to hang me ten times!

Silent now, they follow me, willing to do whatever I say. We reach the machine, they light a flash, and there it sits. Quiet, no paper, nothing. It is under a blanket of cobwebs. It hasn't been working for years. It hasn't been working tonight. And as I realize my error, the horrible pounding in my head ceases. The rattling is over. And the craftiness. I am discovered.

*Finished now, the prisoner dropped the voice and mannerisms of the story's protagonist and waited. Time crept by. No sounds came from behind the curtain. He has discovered me, he thought. The devil has*

*seen through the plagiarism. Fear gripped him in a stranglehold. Then came the voice.*

*"Fairy tales!" it cried mockingly. "Nothing but fairy tales. Stories for children!"*

*"Excuse me, sir?"*

*"Sound familiar, moron?" Satan asked, his tone stern, professorial.*

*"I'm confused. I thought you liked Poe."*

*"You have a short memory, idiot. I, on the other hand, remember all. I even remember reading Poe myself. I remember* The Tell-Tale Heart." *Then the devil began a hurried summarization of that parable.*

*"A man kills another because he despises his eye. He dismembers the victim and hides the parts under his floorboards. But the sound of the deceased heart haunts him, and the villain is discovered through shame. Your story is an eerie shadow of that one."*

*Fearing detection, the prisoner sank in despair. But then the devil issued a pronouncement. "You have stolen Poe's wisdom," he allowed, "but that is not shameful. Ignoring wisdom is the sin, not using it."*

*"Am I free then?" asked the prisoner, a ray of hope suddenly appearing on his sorrowful face.*

*He could hear the devil take a deep, rasping breath, and he knew his time of judgment was near. Then it was upon him.*

*"Like the character in Poe's tale, you have ripped up the floorboards of your life and seen what lies below. You have listened, as each of us must, to our own, personal pounding hearts. And," the devil paused, "you have reintroduced shame to management. Go!" he shouted. "You are discovered! You have freed yourself!"*

*Reflecto passed the prisoner to an assistant demon who escorted him away, then approached the devil's screen, incredulity written on his face.*

*"May I humbly inquire, sir, why this fiend is being allowed to*

*escape? That man is a monster, my putrid prince, a snake! More heinous than I, or . . . ," he hesitated, "or even you."*

*"Was, Reflecto," Satan replied, "was a monster. But now he is benign. Now he has a conscience. And a snake with a conscience is a serpent without fangs. He is little more than a harmless worm. Let him slither away."*

*"Oh detestable duke of the dungheap," Reflecto proclaimed. "Your wisdom is multiplying! You brilliance is growing beyond bounds with each story!"*

*"Please, please," Satan muttered, "tell me something I don't already know, will you? Leave me now, and return with another maggot-brained manager."*

*Once Reflecto was gone, the devil shook his head and mumbled to himself. "I've known him for centuries, and he is my best man. Yet Reflecto still doesn't understand what this is all about. It is not I who needed wisdom—it's them! I am still the professor and I am still teaching. Just in a more effective, and a much more satisfying way." He was still laughing when the door opened and a fresh student arrived.*

# CATARACT WOMAN
## (VISIONS OF A LEADER)

"Come, for only the coward tarries, and it is folly
to look back on the City of the Past."
—**Kahlil Gibran**, *Words of Life*

*After hearing seven prisoners illustrate the errors of management,
the mistakes and malfeasance of modern corporations, Satan needed something uplifting. He hoped Reflecto would bring a messenger
of hope, of heroism—someone who did it right. So even though he
was expecting difference, he was greatly surprised when prisoner
number eight began to speak. The voice was strange. Soft, yet bold.*

*Prisoner number eight was another woman. The emperor of
Hell rose from his throne on hearing her and leaned against the
veil, squinting through the tight fabric for a better view. Something
must be happening up on earth, he thought, rubbing his hands
together in glee. One woman in eight is a novelty. But two? Could
this be a trend? Were the floodgates about to open?*

*"Is it changing up there?" he asked. "Are they welcoming you?
Are they ready for change?"*

*"Some are, some aren't. The bold leaders embrace it. The timid
cling to the past like children to their mothers' skirts, or zealots to a
failed myth."*

*"There are bold ones, eh?" Satan asked, a tinge of skepticism
apparent in his tone. "Do you know, woman, what courage is?"*

"I am courage," she replied.

"And proud, too, I might add," Satan sneered. "But as for your courage, we shall see. For I detect a certain deference, a patronizing air in your personality. True courage means telling people what they don't want to hear. True courage, for man or woman, is facing the difficult truths—to hell with who takes offense! True leadership means taking on the unknown—-confronting the unexpected. Tell me," he whispered, "are you ready for that?"

"I am ready to face my future, if that's what you mean."

"Facing the future is not a sign of courage," Satan proclaimed. "Even cowards cringing in prison cells, condemned to death at dawn, must face the future. Everyone must. But only a few can make the future. Only the courageous can craft tomorrow, bend it, shape it to their wills. The rest are mere passengers on the river of time."

"Strange you should use that metaphor," she offered, "time as a river."

"The metaphor of time-as-river is as old as Herodotus," he lectured her, his face still pressed against the fabric, his attention riveted on her responses.

"But nowhere did the rhythm of a river so dictate the pulse of life as in ancient Egypt," she replied. "Because the flooding of the Nile was so regular and predictable, life was languorous and kingdoms lasted for centuries. Change was a simple annual fluctuation, not a quantum leap."

"I hope your story is ripe with change, resistance, visions, and calamity," Satan warned. "I tire of management error. Give me an original tale!"

She did. She took him to ancient Egypt, to the cataracts of the Nile, and back again. She told him of heroism, and the triumph of the new.

100

I n the Middle Kingdom of Egypt, two cities sprang to life along the river Nile. Trading cities both, they flanked the blessed river on either side and were situated among the high bluffs at the foot of a sweeping plateau. To the left, halfway upriver from the delta to the cataracts, stood Stabile, the first city. And directly opposite was Flux, its counterpart. They existed in prosperous harmony, each providing respite and trade to river merchants in equal measure. Life was good in both, and the Nile was the reason.

Around 2000 B.C., in the city of Stabile, a young maiden was seduced by the king's son and gave birth to a child. But the king, Tradish-on, was outraged. He had hoped to give his son in marriage to a princess of Flux and thereby solidify the peace between these cities. So he acted upon his rage.

The maiden was dragged to the shore and her child pulled from her arms. To a crowd of merchants and rivermen, tavern drunkards and warehouse hands, Tradish-on asked, "What shall be done with her?" And they replied "Throw her into the river and be done with her, for she is wicked."

But just before this was done, Tradish-on himself took the child and raised it over his head and dashed it against a dock piling, then threw it motionless into the water. Next, he ordered his executioner to put out the eyes of the mother, and throw her after the child into the receiving Nile.

Blinded and wailing in grief, the woman flailed the water and gasped and implored the crowd to help her secure her child. And one cruel wit yelled out, "It is alive, and drifting upriver," even though the child was lifeless and drifting downriver, to the delta and the sea.

So the heartbroken woman swam sightless against the gentle

current—calling out the child's name—and after she disappeared from view the crowd dispersed and returned to the alehouses and prostitute warrens and forgot her. Tradish-on, cherishing the example, had hieratic writing carved on a public pillar. "The wicked woman with eyes of cataracts is on her way to the cataracts of the Nile." And he thought the inscription quite poetic.

Life in the cities continued, as always, with the ebb and flow of the Nile. For the Nile replenished the fertile fields all along her path from the cataracts to the sea and made the ribbon of land on her banks lush and green, while all else beyond its flood plain was desert.

The cataract woman swam against the current for sixty days and sixty nights, imploring the darkness for her lost child with each breath. As she groped and pulled the water past her, she came to feel it cooler, the current more swift. The river was narrowing.

She could sense the flow of tributaries as they poured into the great river; and by following the cooler current, she continued to trace the Nile to its source. One morning she arrived at the falling, foaming cataracts, and rested. There she fashioned a humble dwelling to house the years of sorrow and solitude before her. There she dwelled, pondering and listening to the sounds of the tumbling water.

Each year the peasants along the entire Nile waited for the periodicity of its flooding and accustomed their cycles of living to the river's. The cataract woman began venturing in a small craft of reeds downriver from its source, taking short trips at first, then longer ones as she became more skilled.

As she passed the tillers in the fields, they would call out to her. "How long until the river floods?" they would ask. And she might reply, "After Ra has greeted you forty-two times."

Her predictions were extremely accurate, and those who depended on the Nile were amazed at the vision of this sightless seer. But she lived at the source and heard what no seeing person could. She heard the river and its nuances of change. So sharp was her hearing that she could read the water, knowing volumes from the whorls and bubbles and sighs.

One morning she heard a message in the babbling of the small mountain feeder springs and then prepared her raft for a long voyage. She would go down to Stabile and Flux and warn their inhabitants. For the cataract woman sensed what no occupied farmer nor vainglorious king could see. A monumental flood was building. She would give them notice.

All along the journey farmers called out their questions. But when she told them of the portentous catastrophe, they smiled and returned to their work. We know a flood is coming, they told themselves, for one comes every year. Floods are life, they are steady, and they come and go with great regularity. What they didn't know was that there are floods, and then there are floods.

When the cataract-woman arrived at Stabile, she anchored her vessel and stumbled up now unfamiliar streets, toward the king's lodgings. An old guard recognized her from years before and dragged her by the hair to Tradish-on's quarters.

Time had not blunted the king's enmity. Though she tried to warn him of the flood and pleaded with him to protect the city, Tradish-on was unmoved. "This is not news," he told her disdainfully; "nothing is new here. We will not change our commerce nor disrupt our habits. This is Stabile, not Flux!"

Tradish-on ordered his funerary masters to prepare for her disemboweling in the morning. She would be hollowed and waxed and stuffed with papyrus and given to the burial place of the unworthy. For Tradish-on prayed to the world of death and wished to appease Osiris and the minor gods of the past.

He had the cataract woman flogged and imprisoned in a cellar below his palace, near the docks. Her end would come with the next day, with the arrival of Ra.

But as the woman cowered in the dark and the damp, awaiting her fate in accustomed solitude, a sound presented itself. At first strange, but then familiar and telling. She heard water and deciphered its location and direction. Lifting a tile from the cellar floor, cataract-woman sensed a coursing sewer, and in an instant she was in it and traveling smartly to its discharge—the Nile.

Surfacing in the cool evening, she heard sounds of merriment and the push of oars nearby. For the great king Dynamik, lord of Flux, was upon one of his majestic vessels, cruising the river with entertainment and delight. His oarsmen spotted the floating woman and pulled her aboard.

"Feed and clothe her," Dynamik told his attendants, "and take her to our shore. I will receive her in the morning." And this was done.

They broke fast together, sharing honey and bread and knowledge. Dynamik was told then of the impending apocalypse.

"But when shall this take place?" the good king asked. The cataract woman counted her fingers and searched her memory and responded: "When Ra has greeted you twenty-seven times, the river will rise and continue to lift and all the docks and counting houses and storerooms will be covered. The bluffs upon which your city rests will be engulfed. And your people will perish unless they move to the high plateau beyond the strip of green."

This was terrible news, and Dynamik shuddered. For to move to the plateau would cause commerce to cease immediately, and the stay in the desert would be hard and trying for his merchants and their families. But Dynamik believed in Ra, in the sun god, and he believed in the river. And unlike the tyrant across the waves, Dynamik believed in the future. He ordered the city prepared and sent surveyors and scouts up over the bluffs and into the plateau.

There was much grumbling and resistance among the dwellers of Flux, and Dynamik's leadership was questioned when he was not present. One cult objected particularly—the Recalcitrants. The Recalcitrants pointed out the cost of the transfer, the disruption of trading habits, and the competitive advantage the move would give to their rivals in Stabile. So much did they complain and threaten that cataract woman, whom they had quickly come to detest, fled upriver in fear again, back to the Nile's source.

When traders noticed the docks of Flux in abandonment and the people laden with possessions heading into the desert, they notified the merchants of Stabile, who were joyous. "They are idiots," Tradish-on proclaimed. "They take their vision from a blind witch!" And as he predicted, Tradish-on's followers were enriched by the doubling of their trade.

As each day came and went, Flux found it more difficult to sustain his people. Recalcitrants multiplied, complaints doubled, and hardship set in. Ra rose and set, and the river was unchanged. "When there is nothing in sight," Dynamik confided to his lieutenants, "vision is most important."

So they persisted, and the move was completed. Then they waited, in the heat and dust, looking plaintively each day at the thriving city of Stabile across the river. The test grew sterner.

On the morning of the twenty-seventh day, Dynamik walked down to the river shore and looked upon Stabile with regret. We have been fools, he thought. We have gambled on what will be. And there, he continued, there is Stabile—prosperous and content. They have gambled on what is. They are the wiser. Then something caught his eye.

It was a small thing, nothing more than a hickory nut floating quickly by. But Dynamic caught his breath and ran into the river and plucked it out of the current. This is it, he exulted. The omen is upon us!

For cataract woman had knowledge of the plants along the upper reaches of the Nile and had told Dynamik that the hickory bore its fruit on high branches. When the hickory's fruit is swept away, she had said, the flood is imminent. So Dynamik hurried up the cliffs, past the derelict docks and empty storehouses, and gathered his people on the edge of the high plateau to witness the devastation in the river valley below.

And it came, beyond their most anguished dreams. Walls of water roared in from the south, and the banks of the Nile were unable to contain it. The sound of the deluge was near deafening, and the detritus of life, from every village and city reaching from the cataracts to the delta, was carried in its raging torrents.

A many-throated gasp left the crowd as Stabile and its inhabitants were overtaken before their eyes. Then they stood in silence and awe, saved by the foresight of an outcast and fortified by the vision of a great leader.

Finally, immense joy overcame them, and they began dancing and singing. Everyone, that is, except for the Recalcitrants. They were much more somber. They shed great tears and began to melt away into the new city, skulking from sight.

When Dynamic turned from the horrible destruction of Stabile and the remnants of the old city of Flux, he smiled. "To the future!" he shouted. "To the city of the future!"

*"A gripping tale," pronounced Satan as soon as the prisoner had finished. "Very original, very motivating."*

*Prisoner number eight was silent, awaiting her sentence. Then the devil asked a final question. "Was Dynamik a true leader, then?"*

*"Compared to his counterpart across the river, that pig named*

Tradish-on, he certainly was," she replied.

"Wrong!" the devil blasted. "Wrong! Wrong! Wrong! Here I was thinking you were a smart one, and you turn out to be just as stupid as all the others!"

The prisoner flushed with anger and clenched her teeth. Her words came out in terse, sharp bites. "I suppose you could tell me all about..."

"Hold on a minute, witch!" the devil interrupted. "Kee-Rist! Are all of you so sensitive?" She said nothing. He continued, full of self-satisfaction, basking in superiority.

"Dynamik was a good man and a righteous king, I'll grant you that. But the man was a manager, not a leader! A manager gets people to do what everyone knows must be done. A manager controls things, keeps people in line. That he did, but that doesn't make him a leader. That's the difference between Reflecto and me, don't you see? He keeps things running smoothly, he keeps everything humming in Hell. But I, I'm the only one with vision. I'm the one who sees what's coming, what's new, what has to change! I am Lucifer, woman! The Leader of Hell!"

Patronizingly now, speaking as though to a child, he addressed her again. "Now we get to the heart of your problem. You have couched your answer again, you are still frightened to confront the truth! And you said you were so courageous!"

He snarled inaudibly, letting his invective do its work, then roared. "Now, damn you, speak like a champion! Who was the true leader in your story?" Her reply was swift and ferocious.

"The cataract woman, you horny has-been! She came up with the vision, she saw the future, she got people to do what they would never have done without her. She got them to embrace an unknown horizon! She got them to ignore their fears and break their comfortable habits! She shook off their chains, their prejudices, their timid, *stifling self-righteousness! Are you satisfied, rat breath?"*

*Reflecto, having listened from outside the door, sensed it was time to reenter. When his footfalls rang across the brimstone, the devil shouted an order. "Reflecto," he snarled, "take this ice queen out of here before she melts."*

*"Where to?" the helmeted assistant asked. "To your special Hades for Ladies?"*

*"No, No," replied Satan, "to the transfer cell. The last thing I need is another harpie in Hell."*

*They left hurriedly, and when the chamber door clanked behind them, Reflecto whispered to the woman. "He's usually not like that," he allowed. "He's in a foul mood. Normally he's a hunka-hunka-burnin'-love!"*

*She stopped in her tracks and glared at him—a look that pene-trated his protective suit and frosted his heart. Instantly realizing he'd said the wrong thing, Reflecto wisely escorted her to the waiting cell and returned to Satan's chamber without another word.*

*Satan, meanwhile, was considering the woman's story once more; and when his assistant returned, the devil leapt to his feet as though hit by a lightning bolt. He bellowed an order that was heard on the other side of Hell. "Reflecto!"*

*In an instant the acolyte was there before him, his metallic suit shimmering with flame and sparks.*

*"Yes, my malignant master?"*

*"Henceforth, I shall be known by one title only!" Satan pro-claimed. "I am now a convert to change! I am now* the Change Master from Hell!

*"Bring me the organization chart," he demanded, "and the human resources manual, the procedures, the strategic plan, the annual bud-gets, the quality program, and the marketing plan, at once!"*

*"But sir, er, I mean, but Change Master," Reflecto interjected,*

*"perhaps you should go easy on this. There is so much we have built up over the millennia. We have pride and faith in the way things are here. It might be unwise to . . . "*

*"To hell with all that!" screamed the devil. "Everything will change,* now!*"*

*"But the terror of transformation, Change Master, the perils are great, the sinners aren't ready, the . . . "*

*"Make your point, you dazzling dullard. I have a grand crusade ahead!"*

*"Just listen to one more story, master of mutation, er, I mean* Change Master." *Reflecto was begging now, his hands clasped together, his fear uncontained. "I implore you!"*

*"One more story, then. But make it short! I have a world to remake!"*

*Reflecto heaved a sigh of relief and hurried to the door. "Bring in the culture change specialist," Reflecto screamed to the waiting guards. "And hurry!"*

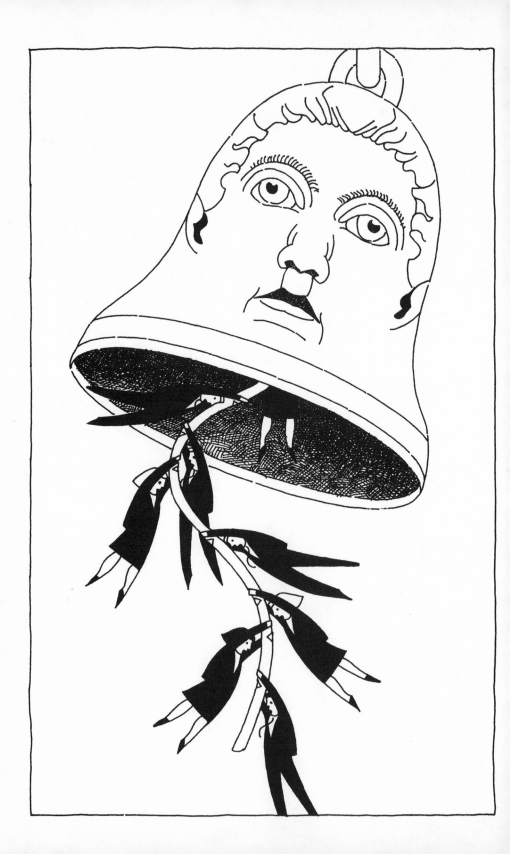

# CONSTANTINE'S CULTURE CHANGE
### (THE CHANGE MASTER FROM HELL)

"Only a few can preserve the just medium,
and neither tear up what the ancients have correctly established,
nor despise the just innovations of the moderns."
**—Francis Bacon**, *Novum Organum*

*"I am an impatient emperor,"* warned Satan, *"and you are a specialist in corporate culture, I am told. I am also told you advised top executives in this matter of change. But I must warn you. I have my own methods for bringing about a new order of things. Shock and surprise will be my tactics. Deep, irreversible, unrepentant change! It is the only way."*

*"There is a saint who would agree with you,"* prisoner number nine suggested.

*"What? How dare you compare me to a saint? I shall have you impaled on a white hot pike!"*

*"Then you would do me a favor,"* the prisoner calmly replied, *"for I would not have to witness crueler tortures."*

*"What do you mean?"*

*"The fate of your organization. The chaos you seem hell-bent to unleash."*

*"I laugh in the face of chaos, stooge! I am the Change Master from Hell!"*

*"Then perhaps you should hear of the Change Master from Heaven."*

*"This I've got to hear! Let 'er rip, reptile."*

n A.D. 324 an aspiring magician of change took the oath as Emperor of Rome. His name was Constantine, and he worshipped the Sun God, had it printed on his coins, and toyed with this new thing called Christianity. In the end, this man imposed Christianity as the official religion of the Roman Empire, and therein changed world history. Pagan temples were sacked, their rituals banned. Thousands were persecuted, and the common peasant had an entirely new set of gods and ideas with which to cope—like them or not. There is culture change and there is culture change. *This* was the ultimate.

*"And now," prisoner number nine paused, "I shall tell the story from the perspective of one who lived it. I shall speak in first person."*

*"Why? What's the trick here?" asked the devil.*

*"First person is more appropriate," the prisoner answered. "All change occurs on a personal level. All change is acted upon and by individuals. You must hear from this one."*

*The devil snorted impatiently, then sat back on his throne to listen. "Go ahead," he sighed.*

I am a humble man, sitting here against the cold and damp, scratching with quill on paper the kind monks have provided me. It is dark outside, in Germany, and I fear throughout the world. This is the new world, then, and I am apart from it. My candle is but a stub, like my life. I shall devote the short length of both to memories. Memories of before and after the change.

Locked and barred inside this subterranean cell, I am a prisoner, but a thankful one. For here my body is contained, but my soul is free. Before coming here, the reverse held, for me and my village. Our bodies were free to work and sleep and walk, but our souls were enslaved. Of the two conditions, I have chosen this one. Bound in body, free in spirit and contemplation. For I am still a man, and men can live no other way.

Theodore, they called me, but not myself, for I was born Thoris, before the change. I was named after Thor, and I swung his holy hammer upon the anvil of the sacred Sun Temple. I was a priest, a diviner of the Sun God's intentions. I read the entrails of beasts and the bones of birds, and told the people when to plant and when to harvest. We never hungered, then.

Upon our temple rose the Sun God in all his glory, radiant in stone and bedecked on ceremonious occasions with wreaths of fir and holly. When marriages were to take place, I would bring the hammer down and the knell would go out and the people would be brought to the temple. And man and woman would be united in love and hope, and the people would dance and sing, praying to Aphrodite and the goddess of fertility: Mother Earth.

Eggs would be placed in hidden places, signifying the anticipated births, and the most prolific creature would be sacrificed—the hare. This was a time of expectation, of a ripe Mother Earth, of birth.

Dwellings would house the Earth Mother, small effigies of her everywhere, with swollen belly, huge breasts, and the joy of fertility upon her visage. She was woman, fecund, a miracle worker, the source of all life. She was like the earth when it received our seeds,

113

and she was as giving. And we worshipped her, and the earth, and the women among us.

For the new season of planting was the time of Mother Earth, of the hare, the egg, and the beginning. Our fields were sewn then, our animals birthed. We would wake to the new year and toil until the time of the great disk, the orange moon, autumn. Crops harvested, our joy secure, we would pray for a mild winter, store provisions, shore up dwellings. And bring forth the tree that never dies.

This tree was another god, for it kept its leaves, was evergreen. In the darkest days, with snow and wind raging across the fields and food dwindling and game vanished, we would look to the tree that never dies and know that we ourselves wouldn't die.

Then at mid-winter the tree would be brought to the temple and draped with candles and ribbons and nuts and berries. This was the time of death. We resolved it would pass us by, as it does the tree, and we would waken again, in the Spring, with Mother Earth. And a new sun, high and warm. And fresh food and new children.

So the cycle took us. Birth to death, resurrection, revitalization, fertility, a great giving forth, a saving, an enduring. This was our life for thousands of generations. This was our belief, since the beginning of time. Before Constantine.

It began in A.D. 312, on the eve of a mighty battle. Constantine had a vision as he prepared his German guards and his frontier armies. He ordered them to remove the Sun God emblem from their flashes and crests and to fight on under the insignia of Christianity. He won the battle. We lost our world.

For from then on the cult of the sun was only mildly tolerated, and Constantine gave huge lands and privileges over to this new church, and proclaimed it the only one. But, of course, living in a quiet village in the forest, we knew nothing of these reasons. All we knew came with the soldiers.

They were ours, and we welcomed them. Then they rode to the temple and drug me from the anvil and struck down the stone relief of the sun. "Henceforth," they ordered, "ye shall be Christians!"

We are a gentle people, accustomed to the rhythm of the seasons and the symbols of our world, and we wondered what import this had. As representative, I asked the lead man. "That is all we know," he shouted down from his steed. "Ye shall be Christians and nothing else!" With that they spurred their mounts and rode over the hill, toward the next village and the next temple.

So we erected the insignia they had left us over the temple door, and continued to pray to the Sun God, and trade in Sun God coins, and worship the Earth Mother and the tree that never dies. We are accommodating folk. We wish no harm.

Then rode into the village another entourage, protecting a visitor. A Christian priest, under liege of a bishop some hundreds of miles distant. "I am Rigor, the representative of the one and only God," he announced, "and you, Thoris, you are dismissed!"

"But who shall conduct the marriages, and hide the eggs, and read the entrails, and adorn the tree that never dies?" I asked, trembling.

"These are forbidden!" he replied loudly, as if to the entire village. "We have new gods now, and new rituals."

"And pray, tell us of them."

"That is all I know." he answered. "I am under the authority of Constantine, and he shall instruct on those matters at a later time."

So Rigor took to the temple and began to make changes. First he took down the tree that never dies and had it hauled to a pyre and burned. The smoke drew the townspeople and the peasants, who stood aghast at the sight. Rigor paid them no heed. "You are ignorant pagans!" he lectured the crowd, "and I have brought you the light."

"But what will sustain us during the bleak times," one cried, "when the howling wind and howling wolves close in, now that the tree that never dies is dead?"

"That is all I know," he answered. "I am under the orders of Constantine, and he shall instruct on those matters at a later time."

As the stunned crowd dispersed, I felt their eyes upon me and the pain of their emptiness. I lifted my hands over my shoulders and indicated no answer and no respite. And I thought to myself, the rhythm is disrupted, and the cycle has been broken.

But then Rigor took to visiting the dwellings of townspeople, and therein he spied icons and shrines to the Earth Mother. In disgust, he swept them from their holy places and shouted that the Earth Mother was a profligate whore. "We shall establish the virgin on her throne," he declared. We wept, and shook our heads.

How shall a virgin bring us fecundity, fertile fields, life of the belly? How shall our women emulate a virgin? How shall our spring begin, our animals multiply, our lives be renewed? Is not virginity a denial? Is it not it a negation of the force of life? These questions I asked of Rigor.

"Coupling is beastly," he told me. "It is of the earth." But this last I knew, and that is why we respected this miracle—it was of the earth. But according to Rigor, it was dirty. "The earth is dirt, and that is bad." We were confounded! The earth was clean, it was good, it brought forth life. Before Constantine.

So it came to pass that our confused and godless people stumbled through one year. We planted and harvested meagerly, with no desire and no hope. And Rigor had the Virgin placed on the throne of the Earth Mother, and dead crosses of planed wood replaced the tree that never dies. We were ordered to celebrate death in the spring, and birth in the middle of winter.

And sacrifices of lambs and ducks were prohibited, but instead we were to celebrate the sacrifice of a man-god from Jerusalem!

Why is it wrong to sacrifice a lamb yet correct to celebrate the sacrifice of a holy man? I was asked over and over. I had no answer, so I asked Rigor.

"Because Constantine has held it so!" he replied. Then I desisted in my interrogation, for the answers were more baffling than the questions. The world became incoherent; the threads of our lives unravelled.

Soon the soldiers came and gathered the young men and took them to fight the unbelievers across the mountains. And the crops failed, and people took to the hills and tried to restore their souls and their worlds. But Rigor had them returned against their will, and many were hung and most were crucified. In tribute, I suppose, to the new god of Constantine.

I left at this time, becoming a refugee on the dark roads, and finally Rigor's acolytes found me, too, and thrust me here, in this cell. And it is just as well, for hell reigns on earth in Germany.

And now factions of this new Christianity have developed. A Christian leader, Arius, has proclaimed that the Son does not share the divinity with the Father in heaven, and so Constantine has called an ecumenical council. And Athanasis of Alexandria has opposed Arius in belief and at war, causing more divisions. Christianity is splintering, and Constantine is even building a new center in Byzantium. Who will win? Where will the center be? And what of Rome? There are no answers.

There is no hope, no future. What will happen to those smiling, gentle people who prayed for children and crops and warmed themselves in the dark forest nights with the hope of the tree that never dies? I have asked the benevolent monks.

It will be over soon, they tell me. The change will take, as it is being enforced by sword and torch. And the earth will never see the bedecking of trees in the midst of winter, nor the hidden eggs of spring. These rituals, they admit, have been expunged. If not this year, then the next. For surely by A.D. 350 or thereabouts, these vestiges of the past will vanish.

But some eves I still hear the sound of Thor's hammer, so late of my heart, ringing through these stone walls and lifting my soul as they chime. The monks say these are bells now, from steeples being erected over the temples. I sigh, and suppose the last remnants of the world I knew are waning.

So I record them as memories, fleeting and ghostlike images and achings. And I accept that when these words are read, in whatever year and at whatever place, Christianity will have erased all and will have been triumphant. For surely, reader, you have never heard of the tree that never dies, all bejeweled with faith, nor the hare and the egg in the spring of expectation. Surely the change is over.

*"This Constantine," asked the devil, "was he such a fool to think he could remake the hearts and minds of the people overnight? Did he not know that wise leaders pull their followers, rather than push them?"*

*"He believed in his cause," offered prisoner number nine.*

*"Yes, of course. But it doesn't matter unless he gets them to believe in it too!"*

*"Do you still wish to become the Change Master from Hell?" asked the prisoner.*

*"I am whatever I please!" Satan shouted. "But of this you can be certain: I will never emulate the Change Master from Heaven!"*

*"Then, dark prince, do you still believe in massive, shocking change?"*

*Satan paused, then phrased his conclusion very carefully. "I have learned from Thoris that change itself is not at fault, for it is a neutral event. When done in harmony with the hopes and aspirations of the people, it is, in fact, good and right. Thoris and his people were used to change—the change of season, the births and deaths, the vagaries of the herds of game. Yet to steal one's visions, to trod upon what has held in the past without replacing it soundly and immediately, and without enlisting the believers in the new belief, that—and not the earth—is dirty."*

*"And what have you learned of human nature?" the prisoner inquired.*

*"I know human nature better than anyone," claimed the devil. "I know the perversity and the pride that affects so many. But there is a stronger force at work on their beings, always has been. It is not perversity or pride. It is* purpose. *People don't live for toil and tribute. People live for* purpose. *You must not destroy purpose without replacing it first. Otherwise you end up with a hellish world, inhabited by lost souls, wandering, drifting aimlessly—helpless and hopeless."*

*"I know," offered the prisoner. "I've seen your organization—I took the tour of your operations. Meaningless drudgery, senseless pain, a workforce of vacant-eyed zombies."*

*"This is Hell, idiot! What did you expect?" The devil scoffed. "I designed it myself—on* purpose! *But we have a saying here in Hell, and as with all our sayings, it deals with fire: The candle can be replaced, but only if the flame is first transferred. If not, the world plunges into darkness."*

*"It is no different with thoughtless organizational changes on earth," the prisoner suggested. "Purpose is extremely perishable. The bodies can be left to do new things in new ways, but the souls are often abandoned."*

*The devil turned his attention away from the prisoner for a* moment, and soon a high pitched wail rose from behind his protective curtain. *"Reflecto! Get this man out of here! He makes me think too much!"*

*"Yes, oh Change Master, as you wish,"* came the response from behind the door.

*"And Reflecto?"*

*"Yes, your Change Master Majesty?"*

*"Knock off this Change Master crap! And take those procedures and charts back to where you found them!"*

# CHAPTER 10

# THE HUNGRY THOUGHTS OF SLAVES
## (THE DANGER OF SUCCESS)

"The danger of the past was that men became slaves.
The danger of the future is that men may become robots."
**—Erich Fromm**, *To Have or to Be*

*Reflecto stood at attention, his new ward at his side. Both were still, waiting for the devil to commence the inquisition.*

*"My assistant has been reading your story over your shoulder," Satan began. "He's a master of the ceiling mirror. He tells me it is exciting, but he also suggests you have composed a sweeping saga—one that spans centuries."*

*"That is true, oh twisted teacher," Reflecto answered. "This prisoner roams from Shakespeare to Julius Caesar. He paints a wide tapestry of sin, splattered with gore. He spices it with bondage, rebellion, torture, gambling, war, havoc, sex—just about everything you like!"*

*"Yes, yes," Satan murmured, wriggling on his throne in anticipatory delight. "Normally we begin these sessions with an interrogation—but not this time. I'm anxious for the story. I hunger for your thoughts, slave. Begin."*

*Reflecto stepped away from the executive, retiring to a bench in the darkness, eager to hear the tale told himself. The prisoner cleared his throat of the sulfurous vapor and began to speak.*

**S**hakespeare has Julius Caesar proclaim: "Let me have men about me that are fat . . . and such as sleep o' nights. Yond Cassius has a lean and hungry look. He thinks too much, such men are dangerous." And the wicked tyrant was wise in this, for leanness of thought and hunger for the future is dangerous to those fattened on the status quo. And it was Cassius' dagger that made his point final on the Ides of March.

*"But what has this to do with the story at hand? What's the connection with leadership, fool?" Satan interrupted. The prisoner was quick to answer.*

*"This: That only those craving the future will lead. The lean ones. The hungry ones. The ones who act out the words Shakespeare gave Cassius: 'No airless dungeon, nor strong links of iron, Can be retentive to the strength of spirit.'"*

*"So, to speak of leaders we must speak of prisoners?" Satan asked, snorting cynicism. "To speak of freedom we must speak of slaves?"*

*"And to speak of all these in Roman times, we cannot avoid one great man," the prisoner replied. "Spartacus. This slave did not read Shakespeare, he inspired the bard. And Shakespeare took note. In the play of Julius Caesar, he wrote 'So every bondman in his own hand bears The power to cancel his captivity.' This is the hungry thought of slaves like Spartacus. It leads to sleepless nights for the Caesars, and new dawns for the rest of us."*

*"There he goes with the Shakespeare, again!" wailed the devil.*

*"This imbecile has Hell confused with a high school literature class!"*

*"That is easy to do," Reflecto offered from the shadows.*

*"A comedian I don't need!" screamed Satan. "I need a story-teller! Get on with the tale, and cut Shakespeare out of this."*

*So he did. Almost.*

It was a time when giants strode the earth. Pompey, the great Roman general, was victorious throughout Spain. Pirates and robbers roamed the seas and captured slaves and sold them to the Romans, who delighted at their bondage and butchery. And the Romans got used to slaves and established a gladiator school at Capua to train these tortured souls to fight. Not to fight enemies, nor for the glory of Rome, but for their perverse pleasure at seeing them slain in amusement.

Spartacus was a Roman soldier, and he thought of freedom constantly. While others resigned themselves to their fate and served Pompey, either as slaves or soldiers, Spartacus hungered for more. He deserted the army and ran from the Romans who pursued him. Alas, he was caught and made a slave. But the man retained his spirit, constantly bridling at captivity. When this was noticed, Spartacus was made a gladiator.

In Capua he was trained, with pike and net and trident and blade. He was pitted against great hulking men from Corinth and Carthage and Ethiopia and Egypt. And Spartacus fought like a lion, for his heart was on fire. He began to draw notice from the visitors to the school, and he began to draw strength from his convictions.

Two such visitors were mere youths, standing against the slave pits and eyeing the gladiators within. Patricians both, they were want to wager on the outcomes of the contests and keen to pick winners in their lairs.

In one pit stood Spartacus, but he drew no attention from the two gamblers. Spartacus was lean, not of mass. The rest were more appealing contestants: great bulky behemoths, chosen for their strength.

Then the visitors adjourned to the practice dens, and watched a few matches. Spartacus was pitted against his instructor, a freed slave named Token. Token would challenge a student combatant and, most times, humiliate him. This humiliation was to embitter the loser, and to make him meaner for the real matches that followed.

In this duel Spartacus was given a dagger and a pike, and Token an axe and a net of chain mail. At first they circled each other before the meager crowd, then Token started taunting Spartacus. "I shall imprison you with the net," he cried, "and we shall see how freely you will fight!" But Spartacus was undeterred, silently circling with that lean and hungry look our two visitors began to notice.

Then Token hurled the net with great effort, it being large and heavy, and it carried through the air and approached Spartacus. But Spartacus was thin and wiry, and he easily leapt into the air and let it pass under him. Angered, Token charged Spartacus, and they engaged in grappling, swinging pike against axe. Suddenly the axe cut the pike in two, and Spartacus was left with a short dagger only.

Seeing his advantage, Token wailed and charged, swinging his axe above his head. Stepping to the side, Spartacus let him pass in his fury, and Spartacus was untouched. "I shall split you in two!" cursed Token, spinning now and regaining his composure. Then he stopped, dead in his place, with a dagger protruding from his belly.

Spartacus had thrown it, at thirty paces, and caught Token off guard. Immobilized, Token was not mortally wounded. As he was tended to by others, Token cursed Spartacus again. "You have broken the rules. You cannot throw the dagger; it is not an arrow. It is for close-in combat only!"

But Spartacus paid him no heed. He was not one to play by the rules, for the rules enslaved him. Spartacus had vowed years ago to rebel against the rules of oppression. He had merely seen an advantage and taken it. "Any slave who sees advantage and doesn't seize it," Spartacus replied, "deserves to be a slave."

The two visitors were impressed, but for different reasons. One boy vowed to support Spartacus should he ever be brought to the Coliseum in Rome for the great games. The second youth wished to witness that contest as well, but only to see Spartacus killed. This slave is too clever, too hungry, he thought.

The time did come, years later, for Spartacus to be chained to a contingent of competitors and paired in the Coliseum. As was customary, all were feasted on the eve of the match, and given roasted oxen and leather bags of wine and food of all types. But while the others gorged, Spartacus ate meagerly, in silence. He was still lean, and wished to stay so. He was hungry, yet not for the scraps thrown to slaves, no matter their taste. He was hungry for freedom.

Then the games began, with ten matches to the day. Spartacus, being lean and swift, went into the fighting pit, first against Hominus, a beast from Egypt. This being a preliminary bout, few were in attendance. But the wily and willful Spartacus made short work of Hominus, and the heavier fighters and giants came next. The crowd picked up.

The two youths wagered heavily, for they had been born noble, with large purses. And when Spartacus stunned the crowd by lasting into the tenth match, they bet each other. For one respected Spartacus, and the other despised him. And the respecting one went away richer, while the despiser went away despising

Spartacus even more. Because Spartacus won.

The spectators were amazed, and word reached Pompey that a thin man had triumphed over the beefier brawlers. Pompey sent for Spartacus. "Have him service my wife," Pompey ordered, "for she approves of thin slaves!" And roaring with laughter, Pompey waved his hand and Spartacus was taken to the royal chambers and ordered to fulfil his emperor's wish.

But though many a slave would have gladly complied, for the wife was comely and gentle, Spartacus did not. He was hungry, but not for the flesh of another man's wife. He was hungry for the satisfaction of his spirit. He was craving freedom. While alone with the empress, Spartacus made an excuse to prepare himself for the night's debauchery and slipped from a window and found his escape.

Through the night he fled on wings of hope and fear. Through the streets of Rome, dark now, save for the occasional lamp of a wine parlor or brothel. Past all he ran, to the edge of the great city, and vanished into the hills. Spartacus was free!

In the wild he found others with similar stories, and a handful followed him back to Capua, to the gladiator school. There he freed the doors to the slave pens, and hundreds emptied into the night and followed Spartacus to Vesuvius, the great mountain of fire.

In the months that followed, other slaves would hear of Spartacus and join him in flight. Thousands enlisted in his conspiracy, and soon Spartacus had an army.

And a ferocious one it was. For all were escaped slaves, and all had hunger for freedom and distaste for the past. All were sure of certain torture and death should they be captured, so all fought on like frenzied demons from Hell. They attacked the army's outposts and made off with weapons and supplies and returned to Vesuvius as victors.

Then the Romans sent out army after army in retaliation and to put down the slave revolt, but still Spartacus and his followers repulsed them and maintained their freedom. Romans from throughout the empire began to follow the exploits of these slaves, at first amused, then stunned, then determined to eliminate them. The armies sent against them were doubled.

But the escaped slaves were lean and hungry; and, numbering in the thousands, they could not be stopped. They attacked in response, and fled when outnumbered to attack somewhere again at some other time. Roman citizens were shocked. They had been told their armies were invincible, and here the rabble was humiliating them. And not fighting by tradition!

Desperate, they looked for a great general to form an even larger army and put down the revolt. But Pompey, their hero, was off again in Spain and quite unavailable. So Crassus, an opportunist millionaire, volunteered to take the standard against the upstarts and to punish them for affronting the tradition of slavery and the property of the patricians.

Meanwhile, Spartacus was experiencing difficulty. His band of revolutionaries had grown smug. They took to naming generals of their own and to fighting over positions and insignia, protocol and titles. They amassed vast hoards of plunder and lugged it ponderously from one camp to the other. And the camps themselves grew to great, solid defensive citadels, the better to protect and secure their growing wealth. And, in a move that would be repeated countlessly throughout the history of revolutions, they quashed those among them who insisted on further change, greater freedoms. They lost the hunger, and they gained the conceit of the satisfied.

We can defeat anyone, anytime, they proclaimed, and they wanted to meet Crassus in an open field and fight his legions chest-to-chest. "That is their way of fighting," warned Spartacus, "not

129

ours. We fight by night, in small groups, the way of the lean wolf. We have not the numbers to fight the way of the fatted bulls." And they argued over many a campfire on this.

In the end, Crassus was lucky. Spartacus' men were so smug and established they began to think like the Romans—vying to protect their booty and establish their names. Despite Spartacus' commands to the contrary, the former slaves gathered for a showdown with the Roman Army. They met Crassus on a field, massing in the conventional manner, challenging the legions of Rome with legions of their own. And, in the conventional manner, they were defeated by superior numbers.

Spartacus was killed, and six thousand of his followers were crucified along the long road to Rome. Thus Spartacus' followers mimicked Rome itself: an upstart gaining success and becoming degenerate and vicious—and vain.

Then ironies piled on more ironies. For Pompey, who had been in Spain, hurried back, cut down the crucified rebels, and paraded some to Rome. And he arrived there before Crassus! Thus Pompey, a bystander to all this, received the laurels and accolades of the offended population and was called "the Great!"

Pompey stood for consul, joined Crassus' party, and the two allied with a third young man: Julius Caesar. You see, Caesar was a gambling man.

While a youth in Capua, he had seen Spartacus in the practice pits. He had seen him in Rome, when Spartacus had defeated ten antagonists in one day. Caesar had bet against him then, against another of his good friends. That being Cassius, with the lean and hungry look. Cassius, who thought too much and didn't sleep at night. And who, like Spartacus, wasn't afraid to break the rules. Nor to use a dagger in an unexpected way.

For that is the duty of a leader. Be it man or woman, slave or free, the job is to take the rest to a land that is different, to circumstances unknown. To wrest the future from the clutches of those who are sated on the present. And to do this you cannot be happy with the status quo. You must be hungry for the new.

You must defend people's right to a future, like Spartacus. And this sometimes means rebelling against the present. For leadership isn't falling in line and mouthing the phrases of those who sleep well at night. Leadership is stepping out, creating new phrases, and being willing to defend them.

Were we to ask Spartacus, Shakespeare, or even Cassius to summarize this skipping through literature and history, the response would be quite clear: Never lose the respect for the bottom rail. Never grow sated. Never think you have people owned. Always encourage dissatisfaction with what is. Never punish those who yearn for fulfillment. Do not expect your leaders to come from the leading class or to think the leading thoughts or to accept the leading ways.

Look to the outcasts, the rebels, those with the lean and hungry look. And if you see them practicing new things and thinking new thoughts, do not bet against them. Put them in charge of your companies, your armies, your nations.

For who is slave and who is free? The person with power and no dreams, or the person with no power but that of dreams? The ones who are fat on the present "and such as sleep o'nights?" Or the lean and hungry, too restless and too full of visions to slumber?

*Finishing this way, with a question rather than a conclusion, was risky, and the prisoner knew it. There was no telling how the devil might respond, or*

131

*even if he would respond at all. Now it seemed his captor was pondering, cogitating, for the prisoner could hear muted sighs and snorts, the sound of a fist being pounded on a table—then a muffled "Ahh-ha!" came through the curtain.*

*"Your sense of timing is appalling," the devil pronounced. "Why did you jump around from Shakespeare to Spartacus and back? You crossed more ground than a professor on amphetamines!"*

*"You said you wanted enduring lessons," the prisoner replied. "Ones that last. And this one is eternal."*

*"Yes, yes, of course," Satan replied. Silence followed. Then the prisoner spoke again.*

*"May I leave now? May this slave be freed?"*

*"Not so fast, toad! I've got one more test for you. A question, really. And here it is: Why did I bring you down here?"*

*"Simple, sir," the prisoner responded, "to punish me, along with all the rest. I was guilty, like Caesar, of placing only the fat and happy around me. Of staffing my departments with yes men, and choosing my advisors from the comfortable class, from those sated on the status quo."*

*"For a man who can write a profound tale, you are as thick as they come," Satan hissed. A sigh of disgust rippled the black shroud. Then he drew a deep breath, like an impatient schoolmaster about to lecture a truculent youth.*

*"I'm not interested in punishing you, fool! Whenever you get a chance, take a look around this place. I've got murderers, child abusers, thieves, rapists, even cannibals. I don't need to punish a bunch of white-collar wimps! I brought you here* to teach you something. *I brought you here so you'd be frightened, on edge, captive—hungry. You would never have written such a masterpiece on earth—sitting in your comfortable office, protected and secure!" He let this sink in for a moment, then continued his harangue.*

*"Sated on the status quo? That was you, dummy! I brought you*

enlightenment by bringing you here. I made you a hungry slave. I freed your mind by imprisoning you. When the chains were clamped on your body, your thoughts were released. Your soul escaped its comfortable cage!"

"You engineered this?" the prisoner asked. "You gave me that lean and hungry look? You kept me from sleeping nights? Just to get me to write this story from the perspective of a slave?"

"What did you write on earth?" Satan inquired. "What important contribution to management literature did you make? What original insight did you produce?"

Silence followed. The prisoner was dumbstruck.

"Exactly my point," said the devil. "When, or should I say if, you return to earth, you will be a more competitive corporate gladiator. I have blessed you with the hungry thoughts of slaves."

"What do you mean, if I return?" the prisoner demanded, full of confidence now and expecting a well-earned reprieve. "I've been sweating my ass off down here! I've lost forty pounds, and I haven't slept for two weeks! How much suffering do you need before you finally achieve wisdom?"

Satan's ominous hand emerged from behind the curtain and pointed menacingly at his assistant, at Reflecto. "For some," he muttered, "it takes an eternity."

They left the devil then, Reflecto frowning at the insult and the prisoner baffled. Outside, while they stepped through the steaming corridor, the executive asked his guard why he put up with such abuse from his boss.

"Oh, that," Reflecto said, "that's nothing. I'm used to it by now. In the early days, it was much worse. He used to hit me over the head with a wooden mallet from time to time."

"What in hell for?" asked the prisoner.

"Punishment," Reflecto told him. "And just for old time's sake." When he detected his prisoner's puzzlement at this, Reflecto quickly added, "But that was another story."

# KILLER BEES
## (HOW CONSULTING GOT STARTED)

"The first divine was the first rogue who met the first fool."
**—Voltaire,** *Essai sur les Moeurs*

*"How many more of these insects are out there?" the devil inquired of Reflecto.*

*"Just two, your malignant majesty. But one in particular appears to be quite knowledgeable."*

*"Send him away, cretin! I've heard enough."*

*"But sir, he may teach us something new."*

*"Impossible!" snapped Satan. "I've heard it all! I know it all! Ask me anything, underling. I'm an expert in business now, a master of management!" Then the devil reached for a stone tablet and began to recite from the notes he had engraved upon it.*

*"I know everything there is to know about power, and procedures. I learned it first-hand from Hammurabi! Make no bones about it—I'm a decision maker, too. I know the secrets of Easter Island, the CIA, and I know that Edgar Allen Poe died in Baltimore. Ask me about leadership, about Shakespeare, or the Shakers. And innovation? Ask me about fast food and Tibet. Or management by participation, vision, consensus building. Bureaucracy and bull."*

*"But sir, one can never know enough," pleaded Reflecto. "I have been listening to these tales as well, outside your door. Perhaps there is something missing. Perhaps we could use a little*

*caution or . . . dare I say it . . . a little humility?"*

*"For what?" demanded Satan. "I'll be damned if I'll apologize for being the wisest manager there is! Why, I'm a change master, a cost control guru—a quality expert. Why should I listen to anyone? I could be charging a high fee for sharing all these secrets. In fact, I should be a management consultant!"*

*"I will not disagree, sir. You could take shysterism to new heights."*

*"Well, then, why bother with this next prisoner?"*

*"He is a management consultant himself, sir. He might offer you a few helpful tips."*

*"Hmmmm. A management consultant, say you? How do you know?"*

*"He has a wrinkled suit, a briefcase, and is more than fifty miles from his office. Why, on the way from the writing cell he even stole my watch, then charged me a thousand dollars to tell me what time it was."*

*"A consultant for certain!" exclaimed the devil. "What the hell. Send him in!"*

*"My story is from the Dark Ages," began the consultant. "But not the era you might suspect. The first Dark Ages, of which few know—except my clients, that is."*

*"Cut the foreplay and tell the story," shouted Satan. "And don't turn on the meter!"*

*The consultant continued, reading now from his brief notes.*

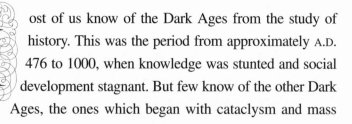

ost of us know of the Dark Ages from the study of history. This was the period from approximately A.D. 476 to 1000, when knowledge was stunted and social development stagnant. But few know of the other Dark Ages, the ones which began with cataclysm and mass migrations throughout western civilization, and during which wisdom was also extinguished. This is a story of those terrible centuries and of that irretrievable loss.

This era began much earlier, in approximately 1200 B.C. In Greece it is darkly known as the Dorian Invasions. Plato later referred to the lost continent of Atlantis, but present geologists suggest it was triggered by the volcanic eruption of the island of Thera in the Agean Sea. Huge migrations and intermingling of previously distinct peoples ensued. Wars, famine, and disruption of centuries-old civilizations resulted.

The Acropolis was in flames, the Nile Delta overwhelmed, the coast of Israel devastated. From Assyria to Macedonia to Sicily, chaos ensued. The fragile structure of societies was crushed, and darkness reigned. Not until the birth of classical Greece hundreds of years later, with Plato and Aristotle and the rest, did intellect reemerge.

I am a management consultant, so, of course, I have a special theory to sell. It was not volcanoes, not tidal waves, nor the onslaught of barbarians that doused the light of thought. It was something different. It was Killer Bees! It began with a man like you.

From Thebes he came, unemployed and without a proper trade. He was gaunt and smooth, however. He dressed finely, and he carried a cylindrical tablet. On the tablet he inscribed the information he collected on his journeys. He called it a "roll-a-scroll," and he guarded it well.

He hailed from a peasant village known as Veneer, and because of his angular frame and short attention span, his few friends called him Thin. As he drifted down to Knossos, on Crete, hoping to find some cretin, he made his way to a wine house, this Thin Veneer.

There, after securing his roll-a-scroll, Thin Veneer joined two revelers at table. One was a wine merchant himself, and flush with coin. The other a solitary sort, by the name of Pythagoras. The wine merchant was loose and buying. Thin Veneer smiled and pulled up a chair. He liked wine, did he, but he loved it more when others paid.

Wine and words began to flow amongst them, and both were indeed fine. "Whence cometh this nectar?" Thin Veneer asked. And the merchant drunkenly allowed that it was from the land of the Hittites, near the great inland sea. Veneer left to relieve himself, and scurrilously engraved this location on his roll-a-scroll. This could be valuable, he thought, but later.

Pythagoras was on a journey from Athens to Egypt, one he had taken many times before. In his peculiar way, the old drinker espoused his own thoughts, with words like hypotenuse, trigonometry, and cosine. Then, off on a tangent, Pythagoras drew strange figures on a wine blotter, all angles and measures. When Pythagoras withdrew for relief, Veneer swept the blotter into his coat.

And the night ended thusly, with the merchant empty of currency and Pythagoras empty of urine—and Veneer full of ideas.

Booking passage to the land of the Hittites, Veneer was off with the morning. There he made acquaintance with a master builder and again sat down with a stranger to sup, and steal. For the builder knew of Hittite wine, as did all the inhabitants, and after he spoke of fermentation, acidity, and root grafts, Veneer made entries on his roll-a-scroll.

"Have you knowledge of trigonometry?" Veneer asked. And he traded his knowledge, late of Pythagoras, to the builder for a huge sum. The builder was excited and dreaming of great temples and elegant public works, all to be had with the mathematics thus bargained. He had more questions, but the night was upon them, and Veneer and his roll-a-scroll were off before they were answered. Veneer was bound for Athens.

In the shadow of the Acropolis, he encountered a public speaker, one Salon. And Salon was discoursing on democracy, government, liberty. At first Veneer took him for a lunatic, but he drew out his roll-a-scroll and etched the notions anyway, just in case.

Later that day he found a grower of grapes, who was to enrich Veneer for the secrets of Hittite wine. But when the grower inquired as to soil types, planting methods, and the use of the prune, Veneer mumbled and lost himself in the crowd outside. To Egypt went he.

At the mouth of the Nile, Veneer ingratiated himself to the servant of a public official. "Take me to your leader," he requested, "for I am expert on governments and this thing called democracy." And it was done. Veneer dined with the governor upon a watercraft, lit with candles and opportunity.

"Tell me of this democracy," the governor began, "for my deputy attests that you invented it and tested it in Athens." And Veneer vouched that this was true and struck yet another bargain. The craft they sailed on was heavy and large, yet floating gracefully upon the waves. How so? he wondered, for most ships are light and small, else they sink. To explain this mystery, the grateful governor introduced Veneer to Archimedes, the wizard.

From Archimedes, Veneer learned of displacements, specific gravity, mass, and weight. The words were meaningless and their import uncertain, but Veneer cared not. They went on the roll-a-scroll.

And when Archimedes and the governor wished to discuss the risks and price of democracy, so keen they were to apply it, Veneer occasioned to accidentally fall overboard in the darkness. Of course, his roll-a-scroll went with him.

So it went, this itinerant charade. For Veneer was lost without luster. His depth of knowledge of any subject, be it trigonometry, vintage, democracy, or fluid dynamics, was shallow. Like a bee, he passed from flower to flower, carrying pollen from one variety of plant to another, yet never knowing what he was carrying nor its implications for the future.

And like a bee, his roll-a-scroll was inscribed with buzzwords. They sounded good, and they were, to a certain, limited extent. But Thin Veneer would always escape with the gold and additional pollen before they could be applied. And in this way, the spores of devastation were carried from land to land. For Thin Veneer, the agent of the apocalypse, the progenitor of darkness, was a man who claimed to be carrying the light.

Inevitably his clients, keen on advancement and desperate for improvements, began to unveil the buzzwords of the killer bee.

In the land of the Hittites, master builders erected great ziggurats using the veneer of trigonometry. In Greece, whole fields were given over from wheat and barley to the grape. In Egypt, councils of government were rearranged, and the pharaoh's staid leadership was threatened.

History is silent as to which event triggered the dark ages of antiquity. Some say it was the collapse of temples and monuments and dwellings throughout the Hittite domain. Some point to famine in Greece, when sterile vineyards produced no fruit, and wheat and barley were fought over by raging crowds of the starved. And, of course, civil disturbances and anarchy erupted in the sedate kingdom of the Nile, with upheaval upon upheaval among the masses.

But by then Thin Veneer, the buzzword king of ancient consultancy, was long gone. His pockets full and his roll-a-scroll laden, he disappeared. Legend has it that he was last seen journeying toward the soon-to-be sunken continent of Atlantis, there to sell his knowledge of Archimedes. There to impart the buzzwords of buoyancy.

Were this the end, it would be horrible enough. But it isn't. For the method of Thin Veneer did not go unnoticed. Certain bands of brigands looked on as he buzzed about, and etched notes for themselves. Like locusts, they burrowed into the earth, only to reappear years, even millennia, hence.

Some killer bees slept until the twentieth century, only to reemerge and infest the world of business and commerce. Not with roll-a-scrolls, but with briefcases and rolladexes—spinning them constantly, looking for a new client to sting.

For that is how knowledge is extinguished and improvement halted. Not with learning, but with leveraging. Not with deep research and careful analysis, but with the purchase of a management fad. And that is how the art of management ends.

Not with a bang, but with a buzz.

*Hearing the end of this frightful story, Reflecto crept into the chamber and stood behind the eleventh prisoner. The devil was commenting on something or other; Reflecto wasn't able to catch it all. His tone was all too apparent, however, even if his expression was hidden. The devil was resigned, perhaps even chastened by what he had just heard.*

*"Take him away." Satan decreed. "Far away!"*

*Sensing an opening, Reflecto hastened to take advantage of the demon's mood.*

*"And the rest of them, sir? Should they not leave as well?"*

*"I haven't decided on their release just yet," claimed the devil. "Besides, if I've counted correctly, one still remains. But this consultant here, why, I just might keep him in Hell out of perverse cruelty."*

*"But sire, your bargain? All stay or all leave."*

*"Since when am I bound by my word, Reflecto?"*

*Reflecto's anxious smile turned into a frown, his forehead beaded* with perspiration. He thought a moment, then spoke to the presence behind the dark veil.

"Very well, sir. Keep them all here. I'm sure you could use their help in running things."

"Reflecto," Satan replied, "sometimes you say the dumbest things. Sometimes I wonder if I should have left you up there with your slide projector."

Reflecto smiled behind his mask. Sometimes he wished the devil had done just that. Then maybe, just maybe, he'd have another chance at life on earth. His imagination took over as he considered the delightful possibility. The parties, the wine, the women. Then a scream jolted him back to reality.

"Send in the next clown!" shouted the devil. "Let's end this pain and suffering!"

Then Satan strode to his film vault, pulled a selection or two, and began to project old movies on the wall of his lair.

Reflecto seized the opportunity—and the prisoner by the arm—and sprinted toward the door like a scalded dog. They were almost through the opening when the devil called from behind them.

"And you, Mister Consultant. Don't forget to give Reflecto back his watch!"

# CHAPTER 12

# AUGUSTINE'S CONFESSION
## (REACHING THE LIMITS OF MANAGEMENT)

"But the doctrine you desire, absolute, perfect dogma that
alone provides wisdom, does not exist. Rather, you should
long for the perfection of yourself. The deity is within you,
not in ideas and books. Truth is lived, not taught."

—**Hermann Hesse**, *Magister Ludi*

*The writing room was nearly deserted now, except for a single peni-
tent who sat hunched over his desk, scribbling in the musty silence.
With his fate, as well as that of eleven others waiting in the holding
cell, hanging in the balance, the final executive glanced alternately
from his tablet to the clock on the wall. Judgement hour was
approaching, and he was struggling with a twisted plot and an
uncertain outcome. Reflecto stood in a pitch-black corner and
called to him across the smoke.*

*"I hope you are avoiding carnage and catastrophe," he warned.
"After hearing stories of frightening times and exotic places, of
pestilence and conflagration, of human sacrifice and terror, the old
man needs calming. Take him to a quiet place, a sanctuary."*

*The mad scribbling stopped. Reflecto continued. "Leave behind
the images of havoc and turmoil. Instead," he suggested, "enter the
domain of the human conscience."*

*"Goddamn it!" yelled the prisoner. The sound of tearing paper
followed, and then several crumpled balls of paper sailed over the
cubicle, bursting into flames as they hit the superheated floor and
disappeared into smoke. "Now you tell me! I was right in the middle*

*of creating this whole Armageddon thing!"*

*"Hey, hey," Reflecto told him. "Relax. Chill out!"*

*"Chill out?" the prisoner screamed. "Chill out? I'm thirty pages into my third draft. I've got earthquakes, burnings at the stake, floods, swarms of locusts, and the four horsemen running amok through the world! Not to mention the fact that if it's not fiendishly funny or perversely wise, I face burning in Hell forever and ever—with eleven other slobs jumping on my case the whole time for shafting them. And now some asbestos robot steps up and tells me to chill out?"*

*"Start all over," Reflecto answered, trying to sound reassuring. "We've got plenty of time. The demon is watching movies in his den, and he won't be ready for you for an hour or so."*

*"Oh, what a relief!" moaned the twelfth prisoner. "I've been sloshing my way through blood, gore, history, myth, and literature for two weeks; and now you tell me to chuck it all and relax, to knock off a calming story in an hour?"*

*"Maybe longer," Reflecto answered. "It depends on how many movies my master watches."*

*"Great! Now tell me, robo-devil, just what kind of films does the old man enjoy?" the prisoner asked, his pencil down and his mind eager for a clue as to how he might satisfy Satan.*

*"Oh, the usual stuff," Reflecto sighed.* "The Exorcist, The Omen, Friday the 13th, Nightmare on Elm Street, *that kind of thing. But his ultimate favorite, the one he watches when he's fed up with carnage, might surprise you."*

*"Oh yeah? What might that be?"*

*"An old black and white flick. One with no violence, no destruction. It's called* Twelve Angry Men.*"*

*"How fitting!"*

*"Right," allowed Reflecto. "The entire movie takes place in one*

*room, with little action—simply dialogue and judgment. It's a pas-sion play of sorts. An examination of right and wrong, of con-science, mercy, forgiveness. You might consider that."*

*Suddenly the prisoner seized his pencil and attacked the writing pad with passion. "Stall the bastard for as long as you can!" he cried. "I think I've got it!"*

*As Reflecto escorted the last storyteller into Satan's lair, the dark-ness and mist were illuminated by flickering lights emanating from behind the black curtain. Then the sound of flapping film, followed by the sharp snap of a switch, extinguishing the devil's projector and plunging the chamber into darkness. They heard the devil scramble back to his throne and knew the time for judgment was nigh.*

*"Is this the last of the vermin?" came the call from Lucifer's cavity.*

*"That it is, oh cruel cinematic critic," Reflecto announced. "The twelfth angry man."*

*"Where are you taking me, storyteller?" inquired Satan.*

*"Sir," Reflecto answered, "his story takes us to the center of a troubled . . . "*

*"Shut up, fool! I'm addressing the mortal. Can't he speak?"*

*Reflecto nudged the prisoner and whispered. "Answer him, man!"*

*"I'm taking you away from all this, sir," the final executive mumbled. "We shall enter the domain of the human soul. But it is not a serene journey, for there dwell all the horrors of nightmares, often looming larger and more terrible. It is a realm of oppression, and escape is not simply a matter of fleeing. We cannot flee from our doubts; we cannot escape ourselves. There is no easy exit nor direct relief from a troubled mind. There is only confession."*

*"How do you intend to do all this with a short story, dirtbag?" demanded the devil.*

*"In two parts," replied the prisoner. "Part one contains a revealing, an opening of the heart to anxious inquiry. Part two contains a revelation, a closing to the struggle with conscience. And as with the most searing plays on stage, few props are required. The dialogue is the thing, all else is distraction. And the dialogue is between confessors, for the word denotes both players: he who confesses and he who hears a confession. I call the piece 'Augustine's Confession.'"*

*"Arghhhh!" groaned the devil. "Augustine. I've heard of him. He's a . . . a . . . a saint." He spat out the last word as though it was a clot of bile.*

*"Yes, that's him." the prisoner told him. "He died in* A.D. *430, but not before writing some classic books. Yet he was riddled with ambiguity, his work full of suggestion and contradiction."*

*"Never read anything of his," hissed the devil. "But I've sat through eleven stories that were also riddled with ambiguity and full of suggestion. What's one more?"*

*"May I proceed, your lowlife?"*

*"By all means," Satan replied, with mock cordiality. "Let the revealing begin. Let the revelation be found."*

He is an executive; his garments speak of that, and his briefcase. But most telling is his countenance. He is stooped, beaten. His face is a road map of travail and attention to detail. He sits patiently in the pew this rainy winter evening, waiting, with a skill developed in many airports, over many years. Last in line, his time is next.

The faint light of the cathedral is dimming with each passing cloud, and even the black veiled widows, nodding to their sorrow, are leaving, one by one. Then the confessional door is opened, and a penitent departs unseen.

The confessor waits for him, now, adjusting his white collar within his black robe. And the other confessor rises and leaves his briefcase and brushes his white shirt within his black suit. They will meet, in a dark box. They will kneel together, with only a coarse veil between them, these confessors.

"Bless me, Father, for I have sinned. I am troubled with guilt, and have come to be judged."

"Let us see in time, my son. Exposition must precede expiation, however. You must first describe your transgressions, and then we will let a higher judge decide their implications. Please begin according to ritual. How long has it been since your last confession."

"I have made two in recent weeks, but I'm not sure they qualify. The first was to a therapist, the second a bartender. I unloaded on each, but I am still burdened. I have come to you as a last resort."

"And wisely, for this is the place to unburden. The therapist would deal only with influences and impressions, with your shaping by the past. And the bartender, in his sympathy, would speak of actions and events, with what was done by whom. Here we will take an alternate path.

"We must speak of intentions, of desires, with why you have done these things. You have lain on a couch, my son, and sat on a stool. Now we will get to the heart of the matter. Now you must kneel on the pew. Please unburden yourself."

"One hundred men and women work for me, Father, and I have failed them. I have been a poor leader, a bad manager. I have not developed them, nor have I gained their love and admiration. I am not fit to supervise. I am not suitable."

"But you rush to your own judgment, my son. You have drawn conclusions without confessing. We must uncover the determinants of your self-recrimination. We must reveal the particulars. What, exactly, have you done?"

"I suppose it is a question of omission, of what I haven't done. To begin, my people are constantly making mistakes and are unable to take responsibility. I have to watch everything they do, and most times do it over myself. If I weren't there to monitor and correct them, they would get nothing right."

"Sometimes I feel the same way. But that is not important. What else?"

"I am not setting an example. My way of thinking isn't catching on. Each seems to be motivated differently, and not at all like I am. When I was a worker, I believed in the company! I stayed at the office until the work was done, no matter how late. I felt my job more important than anything else, except my faith and my family. But my people are driven by interests in sports, hobbies, relationships, current events. I have not imparted my dedication. I haven't gotten them to believe the way I believe. I am not a leader."

"Again, my son, leave the judgments for me and my boss. But tell me, have you abandoned them for their difference? Have you protected and defended them, or simply cast them aside?"

"Perhaps that is my greatest triumph, Father, for I have protected them at great lengths. Why, just this year I refused to promote two women who were not ready for the demands of management. I plan to nurture them, grooming them over time. I don't want them to fail. I care for them, yes, I do."

"Are the hundred aimless? Are they careless or unconcerned?"

"To me they are. They have goals, sure; but they aren't as focused as they should be, and I'm to blame. Some want increased income, some educational opportunities, and others job experience. There is no common ground among them. If one values a chance to learn, another might just as soon have more time off. But my job is to weld these together into an effective unit. I haven't."

150

"I am unfamiliar with this task of management, and I'm not sure I understand the sins you recount. Where do you find the guidelines, the measures of sanctity? Where are the sanctions? In the Bible, the Holy Scriptures?"

"Oh Father, I'm sorry, but we in business follow adjunct gospels. We attend universities and study at the foot of professors. We buy best-sellers and learn the seven steps to excellence, the leadership secrets of successful CEOs. Then we read in-flight magazines and attend seminars and such. Sometimes these are confusing and divergent, but some fundamentals of management never change."

"And what might those be?"

"Effective leaders transfer their own goals to the group. They set examples that are impossible to ignore. They incorporate their vision into the views of every group member. They guard and nurture their workers, developing them through defined career paths. They focus group effort and consolidate group strengths."

"And this is the goal of management, then? To imprint so many different people with the same objectives, and to assure that their skills are equivalent and their views parallel? Forgive me, but this reminds me of the seminary."

"Of course, Father. It is the only way to achieve excellence. It is the only way to assure quality, to advance service, to do anything through others. It's the only reason to have management."

"Judgment again, my son. You are so eager to judge, aren't you?"

"Isn't that due to my training and position? Isn't that what I'm supposed to do?"

"Ah, now we come to the end of the unburdening. Now we come to the second stage, the revelation. And although I am a simple parish priest and naive to the business world, I think I'm ahead of you on the road to revelation."

"Help me out then, Father. I mean, what's my penance?"

"Back up and pause, my son. We aren't there yet. We must explore what you have revealed. And I shall begin where you ended—on the subject of judgment and on your insistence that it is your job to judge."

"Well, isn't it?"

"Now I will give you the simplest answer you will receive from me: No."

"What do you mean?"

"You are not the judge of the one hundred humans in your employ. You are a representative of their employer, nothing more. They are not to worship you, follow you, or even like you. They have gods, saints, lovers, and heroes; and they choose them freely. They did not choose you. They simply chose to work for you."

"So? Don't they have to be inspired by me? Don't they have to adopt my goals, reflect my ideals?"

"Absolutely not, and you are wrong to assume they will. But you have sinned in other ways, although I will not rush into them. They are specific, so I will address them singly."

"Is this going to take all night? I mean, I've got a late dinner meeting and some voice mail to catch up on."

"Leave then, and demonstrate your unfitness to lead. For a leader who cannot ask himself penetrating questions and examine his motivations has no warrant to ask of others, or to provide their motivations himself."

"You're right, I suppose. But I've never read a business book that prescribes confession or self-analysis. They seem to deal with whom to use, whom to manipulate. They give you the impression that introspection is for wimps, that to examine your own conscience is an exercise for losers."

"Relax, my son. I have heard many a corporate captain cry

where you are kneeling. But confession is not an effort to examine others, like your business books. It is an attempt to make oneself."

"Then tell me, straight out, what to do?"

"First, consider your sins. Most are simple. When you suggest that your people can do nothing right without you peering over their shoulders or redoing it yourself, this is your sin—not theirs. You must learn to allow them to err. You are robbing them, my son, robbing them of the experience of mistake—and denying them the opportunity to learn therefrom. This is the sin of prevention."

"What else?"

"You are imposing your interests and motivations on those who may be driven by other desires. They might have to perform to certain standards, but you are vain to expect them to perform *because* of your standards. Let them be driven by their own fears and wants, not yours. This is the sin of imposition."

"But shouldn't we have a common mission?"

"A common mission, yes, but not a common motivation. This leads us to your third sin: the sin of identification. You are trying to get them to be you, and they cannot and should not. They are themselves, each different. Because you work together does not mean you should be one and the same. You are you, my son—let them be them."

"But some of them are not qualified, not ready to move ahead."

"This you admitted earlier, and it causes me great distress, as I'm sure it does them. You have sinned again, though—the sin of protection. You must allow them to progress beyond you, or beyond your estimation of them. Your impressions of them become their bonds, son, and this is unjust."

"It seems everything I do, I do to help them and shape them, Father. Is there something wrong with that? Is it wrong to try to mold them into a unit? If so, then what is my job?"

"It is wrong and sinful to assume oneself God, capable of forming clay into human beings. When an employee joins your organization, he or she does not come as pliant dough waiting for firm hands. Each comes with special and diverse talents, unique qualifications, extraordinary personalities, and varying desires. Your job is to capture this diversity and harvest it—not to weed it out."

"Is it a sin to demand a common culture?"

"Yes, and an abomination to presume you are its designer. You have sinned again, my son. You have committed the sin of homogenization. Now do you understand the gravity of your transgressions?"

"Prevention, imposition, identification, protection, homogenization. Yes, I understand them now. But come Monday morning, when I'm back at the office, I'm not sure I'll remember them all, or if they'll make much sense."

"And that, my son, is where I come in. For now we enter a new phase of the confession: Part two, as it were. This is the time of summarization. I have a way to do this. Would you like to hear it?"

"By all means, Father. I am feeling somewhat lost."

"Have you read St. Augustine, my son?"

"I might have bought the cassette. What has he written lately, Father?"

"Not much, not for the past sixteen hundred years or so. He had some monster hits in his time, though, number-one best-sellers. One such book was called *The City of God*. In this work St. Augustine suggests that perfection cannot be found on earth, in the City of Man. He says it's impossible to build the City of God on earth, that it can only exist in heaven.

"And that is your problem, dear executive. You are trying too hard to build the City of God in your organization; and with all this talk of management and leadership, you're attempting to impose yourself as the architect.

"Allow your people to make mistakes, manager. Lord knows, my people sin. Despite my best efforts, I know it's inevitable. Do not expect perfection. Would I, as priest, like to see my congregation as sinless and prayerful as I? Certainly; this is natural. But it would be unnatural to expect, and sinful to require."

"My time is short, Father, but I must not leave without receiving my penance. What shall I do to expunge these sins?"

"Your punishment is simple, and direct. And it fits the transgression. I require you to read *The City of God*. You will find it obscure, even boring; and this will be good. For you will not want to live in the City of God, and perhaps its reading will remind you that the City of Man is the only place to work. As imperfect as that may be, it is all we have."

"Is the book easy to read? Is it a formula for success?"

"As St. Augustine says in his last paragraph, 'It may be too much for some, too little for others.'"

"Maybe that's what I'll remember, Father, about management. That nothing suits everyone, and it is foolish to try to make it so. Whether it be motivation, interests, skills, or even my management style—it may be too much for some, and too little for others."

"Now you have seen the Revelation, my son! Now your confession is complete. You understand that one cannot manage without knowing the limits of management. Now you are wise, and fit to lead others."

Each confessor blessed the other and stood, and left the dark wooden box by opposite doors, heading in opposite directions. One man in black withdrew under the transepts and into the sacred depths of the cathedral. The other man in black withdrew under the transit system and into the shrieking streets of commerce.

One returned to the City of God. One returned to the City of Man. Both arrived at the proper destination.

As soon as the prisoner's voice trailed off, Reflecto, seized by a parox-ysm of impatience, started chattering to his master.

"Great, eh? Black and white scenes? Little action? Takes place in one room? Dialogue's the thing? Tranquil? What do you think, your excres-cence? What do you think? Exquisite, eh? Perfect, wouldn't you say?"

Satan rose from his throne and raised his bony arms over his head. "Stop that offensive prattle! I have learned enough! I have reached the limits of management!" he bellowed. Then a siren wail erupted from the center of his soul, a piercing, painful question. "Where shall I send them?"

The ominous echoes of his cries resonated through the cavern; Reflecto and his charge vibrated to the power of this plea. Stillness returned. Then the devil continued, his voice straining in anguish.

"Where shall I send them? They are in the City of Sin. The City of God is out of the question!"

Reflecto rose on the balls of his feet, his suit shimmering even more as he trembled in anticipation. The twelfth prisoner stood motionless, a strange calm enveloping him. They each considered the alternatives, the weight of the judgement to come, the fate of the remaining captives cowering in the limbo of the holding cell. Then the answer came.

"I shall send them," Satan screamed, "to the City of . . . " Just then, in mid-sentence, a thunderbolt broke overhead and the dank pit was flooded with light. The prisoner felt blinded; then his eyelids closed and he drifted backwards, light as a feather, unburdened. Silence came upon him. Then the faint whine of twin jet engines caressed his ears.

"And one of the seraphim
flew to me
having in his hand a live coal . . .
and he touched my mouth with it,
and said . . . your iniquity is taken away."
**—Isaiah 6: 6-7**

"And every one of them words rang true
and glowed like burning coal
Pouring off of every page
like it was written in my soul."
**—Bob Dylan**

# EPILOGUE

A pair of billowing contrails appeared over the skies of Denver. Down below, three air traffic controllers stood bent over a monitor, their eyes dazzled by a pulsing signal.

"That's it! That's AspenAir 409!" exclaimed one.

"Well I'll be damned, Wilson! See if you can raise them on the radio."

While the young controller reached for his microphone, one of his befuddled supervisors muttered to the other. "Can you believe how fast that bird is flying?"

"That aircraft is screaming, man. Faster 'n a bat outta hell!"

Aboard AspenAir 409, the executives felt a change in altitude and roused themselves awake. Rubbing their eyes, each looked nervously to the left and right. No one said a word.

The pilot came over the intercom and instructed them to fasten their safety belts and prepare for a landing at Stapleton. Upon touchdown, they gathered their personal belongings and stood in the aisle. Not waiting for the plane to complete its taxi, they anxiously crowded the exit, walking on each others' heels, breathing raggedly on the backs of each others' necks. The craft halted, the door swung open, and a ground attendant wheeled over a mobile staircase. They poured off in near panic.

The pilot stood at the bottom of the stairs while they made their exit, bidding each a farewell, and thanking each for choosing his flight. Most took little notice of this courtesy. The rush was on. They had places to go—and places to run from.

But the final man to take his leave did notice the pilot's flowing silver hair and broad smile. He stopped at the foot of the stairs and shook the aviator's hand. When he did, the pilot's sleeve rode up on his arm, revealing a nasty second-degree burn just above his wrist. And a snappy wristwatch, too. The kind someone might be tempted to steal. If that someone were evil enough.

Standing in the falling snow, his bright silver flight jacket reflecting the many flashing lights and directional signals dotting the runway, the pilot wished this final passenger the best of luck.

"Where are you off to now?" asked the passenger.

"Thought I'd fly to Las Vegas tonight. Got a lot of partying to catch up on—maybe watch a boxing match or hit the races."

"Why don't you let me buy you some dinner before you go, or at least a drink? For old times sake?"

"Thanks, but I'm sort of in a hurry. Besides," he added with a wink, "I've got plenty of fish and wine in the cabin." Then the pilot asked, "How about you? Where might the night take you?"

"Into the darkness," came the reply. "Into this vast wasteland of ignorance I shall go again. After the knaves of business I shall prowl."

"Teaching, I suppose?"

"Always teaching, Reflecto. Always."

The pilot saluted. "Call if you need my assistance, sir." Then he hesitated and added, "But give me a few weeks to kick up my heels, will you? Let me raise a little hell on earth."

The professor smiled and shook his head at this. Then, looking up at the pilot who was about to close the cabin door, he suddenly shouted, "When they left, I only counted eleven. Did we leave one behind?"

"Yes sir. You took his seat. The man actually liked Hell. Said he preferred it there, in fact. Said the inhabitants were more friendly and the work more honest!"

"You're serious?"

"Absolutely! Last I saw him he was asking for a copy of the *Journal* and looking for a good deli."

"The Wall Streeter?"

"Yeah. I think he was a lawyer as well."

When the pilot was buttoned in and his engines whining again, the final executive, chairman of the underworld, sauntered across the runway, all smiles, chuckling to himself. "And who says there's no justice in Hell?" he asked. Then he cackled and let out a deep, fiendish howl that carried over the roar of the departing jet.